A Year by the Sea

BROADWAY BOOKS

new york

thoughts of an unfinished woman

A Year by the Sea

joan anderson

BROADWAY

The Library of Congress has cataloged the hardcover as:
Anderson, Joan.
A year by the sea: thoughts of an unfinished woman / Joan Anderson.—1st ed.
p.   cm.
1. Anderson, Joan.   2. Cape Cod (Mass.)—Biography.   3. Women—
Massachusetts—Cape Cod—Biography.   4. Cape Cod (Mass.)
—Description and travel. I. Title.
F72.C3A73 1999
974.4'92043'092—dc21

[B]   98-37082
                                                              CIP

ISBN 0-7679-0593-8

01   02   03   04   10   9

To my role model and best friend—my wondrously
unfinished mother—who continues to evolve
and transcend herself.
Her wisdom, and that of her mother,
whispers throughout these pages.

ACKNOWLEDGMENTS

I am deeply indebted to my friend Cheryl Lindgren, who gave me *Women Who Run with the Wolves* with the inscription: "Never forget our roots." She was referring to our femininity, which, back in 1992, was tattered and unraveling. Together we formed a group of women to share our mutual plight and attempt to get back to our authentic selves. To these original *soul seekers* and *pathfinders* I owe the deepest gratitude: Virginia Dare, Joya Verde, Joan Daniels, Judy Greenberg, Hazel Goodwin, Julie Hansen. We worked toward growth and change for several years and this story is theirs as well as mine.

Local Cape Codders Marilyn Leugers, Nancy Cole, Geri Appleyard, Loni Ebersold, Marcia West, and Judy Corkum added encouragement and insight as the journey continued. Their feedback is sprinkled throughout subsequent drafts. Still others—the Snyders, Emmerlings, and Bormans—

offered their hideaways and cottages where I retreated to sort out my journal notes and formulate this manuscript.

There are no words to communicate my gratitude to Nicholas Monsarrat, Barbara Curcio, and Rebecca Anderson, three intuitive and discriminating editors, writers in their own right, who fine-tuned each chapter, fussed over my grammar, insisted that I not cut out on the truth, prodded me for more when I wanted to give less. Thank you for being incredible coaches during my literary marathon!

And a special thanks to Hannah Andrychowski, who transcribed notes, typed draft after draft, met strenuous deadlines, and cheered me on, for she believed the message.

Of course this book would not have been possible without the clear and steady vision of my agent, Olivia Blumer . . . her sense that I was compelled to write this book, her faith that I could achieve it, and most significantly, getting it to the desks of Patricia Mulcahy and Harriet Rubin, venerable editors who know the market and were able to direct me to write for it, and special thanks to Denell Downum, who navigated the manuscript into port.

And then there is family: my cousin Judy, a sounding board and voice in the wilderness who prodded me from far-away Texas to finish the job; Wendy, her sister, who stood in admiration and cheered; my sons, who continue to push me toward authenticity, and their wives, whose independence and striving determination to become their own persons within the bounds of marriage continue to inspire me. But most of all I have enormous gratitude for my husband, who gave me license to share the hard truths and sought his own in the process. He never once interrupted my writing time, always ready to read the next chapter with a critical eye and encouraging words.

Many have provided a cheering section from afar: the Geigers, Chertoks, Jan, Dan, and Martha Masterson, especially Pamela Borman, a staunch supporter and good friend who believes in my message and is the best public relations person I could have.

Finally, I was so blessed to find my mentor and playmate, the late Joan Erikson, who committed to the task of dishing out her Eriksonian actuality day in and day out until it took hold.

CONTENTS

There is a tide in the affairs of men,
Which, taken at the flood, leads on to fortune;
Omitted, all the voyage of their life
Is bound in shallows and in miseries.
On such a full sea are we now afloat;
And we must take the current when it serves,
Or lose our ventures.

—*Shakespeare*, Julius Caesar, ACT IV, SCENE 3

A Year by the Sea

EBB TIDE

September

Be patient toward all that is unsolved in your heart
and try to love the questions themselves.
Do not now seek the answers, *which cannot be*
given you because you would not be able
to live them. And the point is to live everything.
Live the questions now. Perhaps you will then
gradually, without noticing it, live along some
distant day into the answers.

—*Rainer Maria Rilke,* LETTER TO
A YOUNG POET

The decision to separate seemed to happen overnight. My husband came home from work one day and announced that he was taking a job hundreds of miles away. As he yammered on about the details, I sat blank-faced, hard-pressed for an excuse not to accompany him. After all, our two sons were grown, the big old family house in which we had resided for seventeen years had long since outlived its usefulness, and my job was portable. So where was my resistance coming from? Why was I frozen, frightened, and full of anger?

It didn't take long to realize my uncomplicated truth. I simply did not have the inclination or the energy to move with him. Trying to start a new life, in a strange place, when the marriage had gone stale was simply too overwhelming. I surprised myself when I blurted out the only alternative I could think of: retreating to our Cape Cod cottage to figure things out. I was alarmed by my numbness, my seeming lack of compassion, but there it was staring me in the face.

Consciously, I wasn't thinking this would be a legal separation, just a little breathing space that would be a sort of time-out, a vacation from relationship. For all intents and purposes, we would be back together again in a few months.

My husband met my challenge with little or no emotion, becoming remote, even blasé. We went about making plans for our futureless future with a frightening politeness, casually announcing the decision to friends who gathered after a garage sale in our living room, now emptied of stuff, extraneous and otherwise. While most of them stood aghast, one quickly filled the stunned silence with "Well, what kind of memories do you have about this place?"

I felt myself shudder as one of our sons began recalling celebrations I had created. Others followed, and the remembering continued until the room reverberated with nostalgia. Just then it seemed all right that this chapter of our life was closing. We had lived hard and loved this place much and, perhaps most important, shared it with others.

As we turned out the lights and flopped onto our mattress, now on the floor because we had just sold the four-poster bed, I panicked about my immediate destiny. Mellow moments have a way of erasing all the others. I turned onto my side and draped my arm around his portly middle, reaching out for I-don't-know-what. I would miss the comfort of familiarity, I thought, snuggling closer to the back of him. He stirred, and for a moment I thought he might turn over, say something, perhaps even take me in his arms. But in seconds he fell into a deep sleep, and I was left to be lulled by the pattern of his breathing.

So many nights I had lain beside him wondering what his dreams were made of, what haunted him so. I had known from the beginning that his childhood was harshly lonely, raised as he was in an alcoholic family, sent away at the tender age of twelve to an Episcopalian boarding school he hated. As we were falling in love, he made sure I realized the strikes against him, the baggage he carried, but I, the ultimate caregiver, was all the more challenged by his shadows. I found a sort of comfort going into a marriage where my role as resident nurturer was already defined, and thought I'd fix his melancholia somehow, lifting him above the darkness he had grown so used to carrying.

But alas, over the years I wearied of his pain, which seemed impossible to exorcise. Too often I translated his emotional unavailability as rejection and began pleading for attention: "I have needs, too, you know," I would reiterate, hungering for connection and affirmation. He would look up from the book he was reading and inform me that "Needs are a roof over your head and food in your stomach. Period." That kind of answer generally shut me down, as well as other remarks that always sounded accurate enough to make me feel the fool for asking. He would trivialize my outbursts with a practical saneness, as befits a pragmatic man who favors semantics. Over the years, being on the other side of strained reasonableness became more than frustrating.

Still, there were a few times when he was actually jealous of me. After a dinner party where I had regaled the guests with stories and jokes, as he remained typically quiet and withdrawn, he said, "You're Technicolor and I'm black and white."

"So?" I retorted. "Why not add some color to your life?"

My answers were rarely that clever, and humor was seldom a part of our discourse. I found myself feeling more and more oppressed by a role I had undoubtedly created. My twisted sense of loving was about giving and giving and giving until I saw the pleasure of my efforts on the other's face, so my own happiness was wrapped up in making him feel good. I think he thought I was nicer when I forgot myself. My needs so often must have sounded like demands that he would choose not to meet. When he did try, his attempts fell short of my expectations. In any case, the joy of living had been sucked out of him, and I had given up any resuscitation attempts.

A relationship to me was supposed to be about adventure, having fun, sharing. He saw his primary role as breadwinner and occasional participant in the periphery of our family life. I would fill the weekends with people and parties, hoping to ignite his spirit, but often such occasions made him retreat all the more. When I would try to pry him out of his shell, his retort would be "When will you ever be satisfied with what is? If it's excitement you want, then go get it!"

So I did, promptly developing a crush on a married man—running away from the intensity of those feelings to a writer's conference in Maine, returning with new contacts to energize my career, signing up book projects, thus burying my personal needs in the glamour of the writing profession. Although each escapade offered momentary titillation, all of them failed to bring me what I craved—intimacy and relatedness.

So here I am, with the only alternative I have left: refusing relationship for the time being, or perhaps seeking relationship with myself. It is late. Tomorrow is a big day. I roll over on my thoughts and sink into sleep.

It was 5 A.M. when I awoke, an hour later for him, and we scurried to finish packing both cars before he took off for his new job and I for a new life. "I can't believe we're doing this," I said, complicating the leave-taking and knowing what could come back to me in response.

"*You* can't believe it," he retorted, through clenched teeth. "This was all *your* idea!" My words infuriated him, as usual, and his body language conveyed anger as he crammed the last few bags into my already cramped trunk and slammed down the lid.

"I gotta get going," he said, softening his bluntness with a smile, "getting on with my life just as you are getting on with yours." I prepared myself for more punishment as he walked away, not even looking back. But then he turned, and his dark gaze, though pained, was eerily peaceful. "See ya," he said, and that was it.

The weight of his departure was stunning. I leaned my forehead on the roof of the car and began to cry, having no other remedy for my pain, and then stifled my sobs when two friends stopped by with a Thermos of coffee, food for the road, and hugs. These celibate wives, whose marriages had grown angry and cold long ago, stood there with longing in their eyes. They said I was brave, that they wished they had the guts to do the same, that they dreamed of being able to stand on their own. I raised my chin and placed a finger under my nose to keep more tears from flowing, wanting so badly to protest. "Desperate" was the operative word to describe me that very moment. I could hardly categorize my move as brave. I had been trained to believe in "whither thou goest, I will go . . ." and now I was running in the opposite direction. Each minute that I lingered was bringing me dangerously closer to changing my mind.

Female friendships have been my panacea, always a salve on dark days. But this time I was in a crisis that needed my full attention, not the distraction friends would provide. Staying with the familiar would only serve to prolong my inertia. And so I climbed into my rusting old Volvo, stuffed mostly with books, papers, unfinished manuscripts, and other writer's paraphernalia, and took off, gazing at the FOR SALE sign on the front lawn. My last stop would be the bank, where I would clear out what was left of my savings, $3,782.42. He was to cover the big bills, but I was to take care of myself, a fair deal, since over the years my writing income had paid for such things as the boys' education, taxes, and most of the extras.

As I drove out of Nyack and headed for the Tappan Zee Bridge, I repeated not once, but many times, "You're making the right move—keep going—you're making the right move." Once I paid the bridge toll and saw the sign for New England, my shoulders began to drop and my back molded into the seat. I was finally on my way, and it felt as though this move had been in the works for a long time.

Perhaps it had. There had been other false starts, times when I had run away on impulse but then learned if you run away too often it loses its dramatic effect. This time was different, monumental even. I had tied up significant loose ends before bolting. I felt suddenly Machiavellian, a master planner, or like someone about to die, putting her affairs in order. The lives of everyone I had been responsible for were in place. I fear sometimes, that in my impatience for my own freedom, I had hurried the boys along, encouraging my older son to take the plunge into marriage long before any of his

7

friends had even considered such a move, giving my own engagement ring to the younger one so the diamond could be made into a ring for his bride.

What should that have told me? If I no longer had a handle on my own happiness, perhaps I wanted to ensure theirs. Their weddings, coming as they did at the height of our disillusionment, served to distract us for a time. I've seen many of our friends get into the "wedding machine," with all of its accompanying minutiae. My husband and I were no exceptions. If we were no longer to experience the headiness of romance, then maybe our consolation prize was to get a brush of it vicariously. I often wondered if that was the reason so many people cry at weddings. They see love and want some for themselves, all the while knowing that such a dream eludes them. It felt good being the proud mama and papa at our sons' weddings, being part of the pageant. Was the hope I held for them the hope I still had for us?

But the magic evaporated as soon as the rice was thrown and it was back to business as usual. Even the cat, who was our last dependent, conveniently died, dropping dead of a stroke in our basement one Sunday while we were at church. Nothing seemed to be holding us together anymore.

My head was spinning as I careened onto the Merritt Parkway, and I reached for a pen to jot down my thoughts. "One of these days you're going to die writing in the car," a good friend once warned. "I know, I know," I said, never heeding her warning.

* * *

Cocooned in my Volvo, heading away from everything that was, I now find myself thinking more clearly, feeling miraculously light. I tune the radio to a classical station playing Vivaldi's *Four Seasons*, music I used to run to, a good omen, as I am running to a new life. I once heard that Olympic coaches play baroque music in the locker room before big meets to quell their athletes' anxiety. I take a deep breath and wish for such a calm to overtake me.

Still, I feel naughty, even bad. The one who leaves is always wrong, while the other partner, who passively goes along, gets all the sympathy. Most men, I've noticed, are reluctant to walk out. They may want out of their marriage, but set it up so the wife actually does the walking. Surely, when the boys begin to question what is going on, they will worry far more about their father than about me. They have rarely seen his faults, perhaps because his usual persona is rational, responsible, honest. I, on the other hand, am the one who flails, who has the big mouth, the outrageous moods, who ends up screaming at situations—but rarely at the man who might have caused them.

I'm barreling north now on Interstate 95, far away from anything that resembles city, speeding to the racing violins in the allegro portion of Vivaldi's "Spring." Yet, I can't get away from the negative voices that say I am a spoiled brat. After all, my husband is not a wife beater, he's never called me a bitch (although he has called me bitchy), and he seems so forlorn. "You've really done it this time, Joan!" I say, hitting the steering wheel as if to smack myself. I wish I could have a drink, or some Valium, or even a punching bag!

Just then I am distracted by a sign: NEW HAVEN. God, I've passed this place hundreds of times and never bothered connecting it to my past. This is where we met. Yale was the beginning. I slam on the brakes and skid onto an exit, hellbent on seeing the past, finding an old haunt or two.

In minutes I'm staring at the White Tower Diner, right across from the Green, where free refills of coffee had kept us talking long into the night when we were first discovering each other. Trusting my rusty memory, I turn onto Trinity and see the Drama School, its garish red doors just as I remembered them, and nearby, the alleyway where we used to neck. A couple of kids are leaning against the stone wall doing much the same thing. I drive around the block and spot the dump of a house where I had a basement apartment and where we dry-humped but didn't dare try much more.

There is purpose and excitement everywhere, just as there should be in autumn at the beginning of a school year. I see students with beautifully scrubbed faces, some in spirited conversation, others walking with jaunty determination toward class. Just like us back then, except I suddenly remember his running away when our relationship was getting serious. Perhaps I should have let him go, but I was determined to get a husband, and he seemed a most likely candidate. So I chased him until he caught me, and soon thereafter we were engaged, with a ring handed to him by his mother, given to me moments later. An "arranged marriage" it was, or so it seems as I think back on it now. I had already known he had brought other women home, but as far as his mother was concerned, I had taken the prize. My mother, on the other hand, was duly impressed because he was the son of a doctor, therefore well heeled. She overlooked his parents' heavy drinking in favor of the fancy house and beach club, stuck as she was on appearances, hardly the best manure to spread over a marriage bed.

A car behind me honks as I stall at a green light. I turn the ignition key and gun it, lifting a finger at the guy's impatience and remind myself that I'm trying to move forward and leave the past behind. Once on the highway I open the car window to let the air blow through my hair and feel a rush as I begin speeding toward my future.

I never feel legitimately in New England until I've crossed the border from Connecticut to Rhode Island. That's when I become giddy, excited even, knowing the journey's end is only a couple of hours away. Going home or to a place that feels like home evokes an unmistakable aura of settledness. The Cape permits such feelings because it's where I've spent every summer since I was a child.

A new beginning in an old place. I like the sound of it. Posted over the sink in our cottage is a Wendell Berry quote: "If you don't know where you are, then you don't know who you are." Once there I always feel more secure about who I am, perhaps because its well-worn paths are familiar to me. What's more, I can indulge in a kind of knowing that doesn't involve my head but rather engages my senses. There is not a channel or dune or marsh that is not associated with a time or event or person from my past, and I think I am counting on these memories to remind me of who I was before—that raw-material person I seem to have lost.

I suppose it became truly home after my father died and was buried in the cemetery beside the First Congregational Church, circa 1746, along with one grandfather, two grandmothers, an aunt, and a cousin. I was startled at first upon seeing the gravestone marked ANDERSON, but soon thereafter felt somehow grounded by it. All the other towns and cities in which I had previously resided became mere temporary stops on my way home.

Change occurs slowly on an elbow of land where there is just so much earth surrounded by sea. I know where to find huckleberries in August and bittersweet in September, where the sand dollars nestle and the starfish cling. Even my feelings of anticipation about getting there are no different than they were years ago when my brother and I sat huddled in the backseat of our father's old Buick, watching for the telltale signs that indicated arrival was imminent. First we'd notice the soil at the edge of the highway turning sandy; then spot a gull or two hovering overhead; eventually we'd see the Sagamore Bridge, gateway to our paradise. Once over and onto the other side, we'd open the windows, rain or shine, sniff the moist air with its aroma of dried pine needles, knowing that before long we'd be wending our way through town, past the church whose steeple bell rings every hour, past the soda fountain across the street where we would slurp coffee frappes, past the harbor where our little boat is moored, and finally to the sandy trail that leads to our cottage door.

Lost as I am in my thoughts, I am startled to actually see the bridge so soon. It seems as though I've just left New Haven, and it is barely noon! The sun is welcoming, yet I feel as disoriented as a gull circling overhead before a storm,

uncertain where to put down. I seem to want to delay land-
ing, settling in too soon. I remind myself that I have no
schedule. After all, no one is at the cottage waiting for me.
That thought alone creates anxiety. I'll head for the shore,
give myself time to ease into the move here, and think what it
might mean—let the rhythm of the ocean cradle me and
bring me to a state of simply being.

Once in the parking lot of my favorite beach, I slip out
of my shoes to feel the moist sand on my feet and then run
to the top of a dune as if to claim my territory. Since I am
wholly unprepared for what comes next in my life, I am
forced to content myself with that which is before me. I
think it was Thomas Merton who said that the easiest way to
rid yourself of neurosis is to surround yourself with nature,
or more specifically trees. "You can't be neurotic in front of a
bunch of trees," he claimed; nor, I hasten to add, in front of
dunes or sea or humble scrub pine. Standing here at the edge
of the world shows me how exaggerated my own emotions
seem to be. This strong, silent place interrupts confusion,
rage, and depression, and just now I feel more at home with
the landscape than with people.

I'm staring at the autumn-brown beach, taking in the
aging white lighthouse towering to my left, the gently lapping water to my right, and under my feet the sienna-stained
dune grass. Circling my head is a monarch butterfly, which
long ago should have been on its way to Brazil. "Perhaps you,
too, need some extra time by the sea," I say, as it flaps its
wings and settles on my shoulder. I eventually wander down
from the bluff toward the calm surf, where the water is not
going anywhere, neither coming in nor going out, ebb tide, I

suppose—the sea at a standstill, as am I. It was always the nothingness of ebb tide that drove me to distraction—when the wind stopped breathing and the water was still—when there wasn't enough depth to have a good swim and not enough current to make it a challenge.

High tide was the one my cousin and I liked best. Her family owned a cottage at the edge of a marsh near a wonderful channel that wound its way out to the open sea. When we were kids, it was there that we would swim, but only when the tide was just right, when the whitecaps were churning and the ocean was charged with energy. We would run to the end of a very long jetty, plunge into the cool salt water, and let the current carry us all the way back to her cottage door.

On stormy days, when the boat traffic was light, we would slip off our bathing suits and skinny-dip, letting the rush of water and sea lettuce caress our bodies. Our glee was punctuated with high-pitched squeals as one or the other hit a cold spot or chanced a foot on the sandy bottom, where crabs lay in wait to nibble on our toes.

We tolerated low tide only because it provided us with plenty to do in the way of shelling and clamming or just general mucking about. But it still beat ebb tide, when you couldn't do anything but sit passively by and watch while the sea turned itself around. It occurs to me, just now, that perhaps ebbing can be a rest time, a "psychic slumber" from a lifetime of learning to be a woman. I never thought about just being still, caught up as I was with escape and all it entails.

I'm tired of swimming upstream, against the current, only to arrive at unnatural destinations with little sense of where to yield, when to sow, what to ask, how to find. More than anything I wish to be carried out with the surf and be buoyed by the salt water. But reality keeps me beached for the time being. I need to hunker down like a nesting crab or a plump clam and take stock while the tides wash over me.

It is eerily quiet. My soul is as drab as the September beach upon which I sit. I must be still and listen to the primitive squawk of birds and breathe, breathe deeply of the moist, clean air and be open to whatever comes my way.

2

THE CALL OF THE SEAL

Early October

*When one is freshly informed, has a serendipitous experience,
one's mood is changed, one's heart is changed. That is why
taking time to see, hear, be present to images and language that
arise from new experiences have the power to change one
from one way to another.*

—*Clarissa Pinkola Estés*, WOMEN WHO RUN
WITH THE WOLVES

I*t is* morning—an early, dark morning. I listen for the birds who usually begin chattering at four-thirty. There is silence, only the pitter-patter of rain hitting the skylight above my bed. Do I roll over and fall back to sleep or get up? This is always the dilemma.

I've been here for three weeks now, one day folding into the next. Without goals or routine, I am losing track of time. There isn't even a calendar around in case I want to know what day it is—but I don't. Still, I fight playing the dilettante. My instinct tells me to lie low, to process the grief that is the partner of change, but I am also aware that I should begin to do something.

My only regular undertaking is a daily trip to the post office, where I hope to find a check or two, this being royalty month. With no new projects in the offing, I'm counting on my old books to carry me for a while. The postmistress, whose cat ZipCode lounges on the counter, knows me as both a writer and a summer person. She's mystified that I am back in town, imagining that I'm working on some sexy novel.

A new kind of loneliness is setting in as I lie here with flicker-flashes of hard truths, failed beginnings, mostly dark thoughts that come after phone calls from my husband reminding me of some family matter or friends inquiring about my well-being. With no pat answers for anyone, I'm left frustrated after the calls. Contacts with the world I've left behind confuse me and make getting up not terribly appealing.

Long ago I lived for such rainy days, when I would make myself a cup of cocoa, climb back into bed, snuggle under the comforter, and just listen to the storm outside. Perhaps I would benefit from doing the same today. Recently, when I sought counsel from a minister friend, she affirmed my conclusion that I was stuck. "You're in the desert," she said, "and you're parched, but not dried out." As she talked, I pictured myself sitting on a stump in the middle of a vast wasteland, surrounded by nothing save miles of adobe-colored, hardened soil, with no escape route in sight. "You've no alternative but to simply sit still and listen. In time you'll hear the answers."

I swing my legs over the side of the bed and get up carefully. My lower back has seized up in the past few days. I'm not surprised, as a massage therapist once told me we store our visceral energies there. It has been a long time since I've indulged in earthy desires. It figures that my back should rebel.

My bare feet on the cold floor awaken what vestiges of me are still asleep, and I head for the kitchen and coffee. Alas, the coffee can is empty. I have been living off the staples in the pantry, avoiding the grocery store, turning my back on any reminders of domesticity. But now I want some coffee, and the only place to get a cup at this hour is Larry's PX, a fisherman's hangout. I've been wanting a legitimate excuse to go there for years, and now I have it. I pull on jeans and a tattered blue sweater retrieved from the floor beside my bed, grab the car keys, and head out.

A pea-soup fog makes the ten-minute drive fifteen, but the parking lot is as welcoming as a lighthouse, loaded as it is with pickups, fishing gear, and faithful dogs waiting on the front seats for their masters.

My entrance halts all conversation. I pretend not to notice, and breathe in the smell of simmering bacon. The only available seat at the U-shaped counter is at one end, and I slide onto the revolving stool, plopping myself beside a burly man with a permanently tanned face and a thick, blond beard. I feel awkward barging into a locals' hangout, but a morning fix is a morning fix. The waitress is quick to pour me a cup of coffee while I lose myself in the simplicity of the place— starch-white walls, red linoleum counters, plastic-covered plates holding stacks of doughnuts, copies of the local paper piled neatly nearby.

In a minute or two the chatter starts up again, and I bury my head in the menu, pretending not to listen. They are talking about weather and catches and the poisoning of seagulls, when someone brings up the subject of seals crowding the harbor. I order a couple of fried eggs in order to hear the rest.

Seals here? Couldn't be, but the locals go babbling on about how they number a thousand, and they're eating up all the fish! I look up now, my head bobbing from one fisherman to another, as if I am watching the ball at a tennis match. They know I'm listening. Perhaps they are starting to embellish, I don't know, but their conversation has got to be the best show in town.

Seals belong in Baja or Patagonia, exotic places, not in my little fishing village. I am fascinated as they talk of gray seals and harbor seals and how they used to migrate back and forth to Nova Scotia. But now they seem to be sticking around right through the winter, and it's bugging the fishermen. My cheeks burn with excitement. It's as if someone has plunked a package down in front of me that I can't wait to tear open.

I stop eating and drinking, not wanting my chewing or swallowing to interfere with my hearing; I picture a sea full of seals, and suddenly I want to be swimming with them. Ridiculous as it sounds, I am more than intrigued, I am crazed. I need only a way to get out there. Without missing a beat, I muster my nerve and promptly ask the guy next to me if he'll take me out.

"You're kidding?" he says, taking a gulp of coffee. I stare back with a determined look, although I surprise myself that I am being so bold. "Y'mean today?" he drawls, turning on his swivel stool to the man sitting next to him as if to get some confirmation that he's hearing right.

"I'll be out there for seven or eight hours," he continues, sure, I suppose, that this information will dissuade me. "Gotta see how long I can make the tide last," he adds with a wink. The last comment really gets to me. Imagine timing my day not to a clock but to the cycles of the sea! "All right by me," I answer.

Everyone around the counter is watching our exchange, ready for the next move—his or mine.

"Y'best get yourself some warm clothes and a sandwich," he suggests, calling my bluff. But I don't flinch. "Meet me at the pier in half an hour. The name of my boat is *Seal Woman*."

I shove my plate aside, leave a couple of dollars on the counter, and tear out, racing home in record time, where I grab a jar of peanut butter and a stale bagel, throw a slicker, a towel, and another sweater into my canvas bag, and hurry back to the pier with just minutes to spare.

"You made it," he says, sounding surprised, as if it were all just a big tease. "Toss me your gear and hop aboard."

I'm suddenly tongue-tied, blushing even, as he offers me a hand and helps me onto the deck. I'm shocked at how his touch electrifies me. Has it been that long since I've been touched?

Get a grip, Joan, I think as clouds of doubt quell my adventuresome spirit. What the hell am I doing, going off with a total stranger? I look around at the other boats, also readying themselves for a day at sea, and take note of a grin on the face of the fisherman in the next slip. Nothing goes unnoticed in small towns, particularly in the off-season. I wonder what kind of a scandal I'm starting. I don't even know if this guy is married or not. Well, I still am, I remind myself, although I'm finding this ruse fun. Yes, fun—the "F" word, my friends and I would call it, chiding one another to make sure to have some fun each day. We rarely succeeded; the needs of everyone else always got in the way.

It occurs to me that I've picked up this man! Unbelievable at my age, and yet why not? I remember picking up only one other guy in my entire life, an "older man" I got to talking to on a flight from New York to Dallas/Fort Worth. He offered to drive me to my hotel, as he was renting a car and I was not. When we got to the Hertz desk, however, and I double-checked the location of my hotel, he was headed for Dallas and I was going to Fort Worth and that ended that. The only other pickup, which also fizzled, began on an international flight after I got bumped up to first class; I was seated beside a man who looked like a football player I had dated in high school. We talked all the way across the Atlantic, to the dismay of those sitting around us, and planned to have dinner at some point during our mutual stays in Seville. But his unconsummated business deal got in the way of his having a free dinner slot.

"Would you untie that knot?" my clamdigger asks, breaking into my daze. "Sure," I say, eager to please. I perform the task like a well-trained deckhand as he puts the key into the ignition and the motor starts up. "I don't even know your name," I say, extending my hand. "I'm Joan."

"I'm Josh," he says. "Joshua Cahoon."

We glide out of the harbor with an escort of gulls overhead flapping their wings. Two white herons, perched on a piling, turn their heads in our direction with neither fear nor interest. It appears we are headed toward a long strip of sand held together by a dome of sky. I suddenly feel the pleasure of being exactly where I want to be. My heart is racing. I can barely recall when last I relinquished control to another— took a dare, really, and went off to a place I didn't know, trusting a stranger to take me there.

Once we clear the channel, he cranks the engine and motions for me to take protection behind his tiny windshield in a space big enough for only one. We stand shoulder to shoulder, and I get a sense of his well-built chest and broad back and feel another charge. Oh, God, how pathetic! Even so, I confess that I find him sexy. After my years of living in the white-collar world of pin-striped suits, horn-rimmed glasses, and *The Wall Street Journal*, a rough-hewn type is quite appealing.

I might have a WASP name, but I could never quite behave like one. Such a persona demands that one be demure, pale, thin-lipped, expressionless. I remember seeing Catherine Deneuve in a movie for the first time, and I wanted to be just like her. I tried on her mannerisms all the way home from the theater, acting cool, composed, delicate, like the petals of a soft coral rose, and even attempted to draw my husband out, to get him to do whatever I wanted, the way Catherine could always do with the men in her movies. But I failed miserably.

I must have been a lusty barmaid in a past life—probably lived in some Mediterranean town where the seafaring men were hard-drinking and tough, yet full of bravura and humor. Perhaps that's why I love being here right now. I need to be more wild and earthy.

The combined sounds of wind and the engine make talk impossible. I stare at his large strong hands as they grip the wheel and peek at his cool blue eyes, squinting now as we face an orange ball of sun. His boat is humble yet sturdy. It has the barest essentials, yet it gets the job done. Fishermen don't indulge in excess. They can't afford it. This impresses me. Men who make do undo me. They remind me of my father, a frugal genius who could make anything out of nothing.

We are flying over the surface of the water, bucking wave

after wave. I'm not sure whether I'm running away again or simply taking myself to a momentary refuge. Who cares? The adventure is intoxicating. It amazes me how my perspective changes when I'm in a boat looking back toward the shore. Out here are myriad invisible paths that only Josh seems to know, and we're free to move at whim. No clutter, no control, no boundaries, no societal constraints.

In the distance I spot an island, a grand mound of tan rising from nowhere with a darkened spot in its center. Within minutes Josh cuts his engine. "There," he whispers, pointing straight ahead. And then I see them—hundreds of beached blimps, smooth blobs of gray, brown, and beige, bespeckled creatures that blend into their space.

"How close can we get?" I ask. Just then a whiskered face pops up from beneath the sea. "Is this close enough?" Josh asks.

"Hello," I say spontaneously. It seems a natural reaction to speak back to a face that holds my gaze, eyes never blinking. And then, just as quickly as the seal has appeared, it disappears under the water, reemerging some fifty feet away, looking back to see if I'm following. As the motion of the water pushes us nearer to shore, several of the colony begin to stir, raising their heads, sniffing and surveying. Finally a large bull rolls over, stretches out his plump body, and awakens another. Like dominoes, one after the other turns over until the once-velvety blanket that covered the beach comes to life. *Thud. Thud. Thud.* The sound of hundreds of flippers crossing the hardened sand is thunderous, and I get goose bumps. They begin sliding off the embankment, where they seem awkward and unsure of themselves, and into the crisp, blue water, where they are sleek and in control. They swim to us, curious about our boat as well as our intentions, bobbing up and down like jack-in-the-boxes. Each time they surface, they make eye contact, then crane their necks, as if to say, "Follow me." I am transfixed.

Joshua breaks the spell. "Time for you to disembark," he says abruptly.

"What? You must be joking," I blurt out.

"You can wade in from here," he continues. "They're used to the occasional visitor."

"You're leaving me here . . . alone! I thought you were going to clam?"

"I go on down to the point—that's where the flats are. Like I said, I'll be back when the tide changes."

There is no arguing. I've signed on for the day and whatever it may bring. I quickly roll up my jeans, straddle the side of the boat, and splash into the icy-cold water. "Neatly done," he quips as he hands me my stuff. "See ya in a bit," and with that he puts the boat in reverse and takes off.

Yeah, sure, I think. Judging from the angle of the sun, it couldn't be more than eight or nine in the morning. With the tide still high, it'll be at least eight hours before he's back. And yet isn't that what turned me on? Spending a day timed to the tides?

I plow on, holding my canvas bag above my head. Fortunately the water grows shallower— Oops. I hit a drop-off. Now I'm wet up to my crotch. Damn him! You'd think he could have pulled closer to shore. Jeans were a dumb thing to wear. They don't stretch, they cling, and they're heavy. I should have stripped them off back on the boat, but that would hardly have been appropriate in front of a stranger.

Finally, my last step. I reach the embankment and collapse on the shore to catch my breath, overcome by the primitive beauty of this place that has no edges. For sure, I've been stuck in worse places. I think it's going to be a good day. In any event, I'm quickly learning to relish whatever comes to me by chance.

3

SEAL SENSE

Same Day

Animals may aid us in our everyday lives, in our dreams, medi-
tations. Since they were created before humans, they are closer to THE
SOURCE and can act as allies, guides and familiars
in our search for wholeness.

—An Inuit woman

I*t is* one of those Indian-summer days when you are lured to the shore for one last taste of summer. Yet today I have come for other reasons, without beach chair or umbrella, and suddenly feel as though I don't belong. I am a misplaced person, unceremoniously dumped with a colony of seals on a strange stretch of beach.

I don't know what I had expected. Come to think about it, I didn't have time for any preconceived notions. For once I had acted on impulse and am now left to deal with the consequences. I feel strangely alone, wishing for Josh's company. Do I want to have a fling with him? I don't think so, although perhaps I'm hoping for a flattering spark.

I'm not ungrateful to be here. God, no! This has got to be the most extraordinary beach in the whole world, and what's more, hardly anyone knows about it! When will I ever learn to accept what is given instead of always yearning for more? My lavish expectations too often tarnish my blessings. Right now the seals, at least forty of them, are staring me down as they tread water. I suppose they want me to move so they can reclaim their space and sun themselves. Never comfortable in the role of intruder, I give up this spot to explore the rest of the island. My mother taught me well the importance of accommodation. I developed the knack for selfless behavior because we moved so many times when I was growing up. "The way to fit in," she would say, "is to play by their rules, ask questions, and contribute something." I mastered her advice, since I was forever the new kid on many different blocks, constantly giving, in order to be accepted.

It's getting hot, and I'm sticky. I need to peel off my wet jeans, now thoroughly caked with sand. I place them on a clump of dune grass to dry out and grab my lunch. As I spread peanut butter on my bagel, I wish it were a turkey club with avocado and sprouts. Here I go again, never satisfied with the blessings before me. Of course, I could have come better prepared, but too often I've used up precious time *preparing* for experiences rather than just having them. I must learn to surrender to the moment, but the very word "surrender" evokes giving up and giving in, not an easy task for a demon planner like me, who has spent the better part of my life stage-managing everyone else's show while waiting in the wings for my own time to come. Yet look what happened! Destiny won, as it always does. I'm no longer in control of my marriage, the children, or my future. Nothing is certain.

Actually, there is a sense of relief in admitting that everything is out of my control. It's hard trying to be right all the time, to be a good girl. On occasion being dead wrong and human offers some solace. I'm reminded of the last time I got a speeding ticket. The moment I spotted the patrol car, its lights spinning in my rearview mirror, my heart sank. I quickly took my foot off the gas pedal, not wanting to admit to speeding, and pretended that it wasn't me he was after. But when he turned on the sirens, I knew I had to ditch the charade. I'd been caught, and giving up was the easiest alternative.

Perhaps I've held on to control out of fear that if I didn't, the whole family would go down the drain. I've been labeled strong, even resilient, two admirable traits that have been my undoing. But one day I caught on to the burden that goes with control: The controller does most of the work! Oddly enough, it was just this quality that attracted my husband to me. "I never thought I would need to take care of you," he said nonchalantly, twenty-five years into the marriage, as I stared utterly dumbfounded at him. "You've always appeared so strong and in control." Ever since that statement, I've come to despise being called strong, being the one everyone counts on to pick up the slack.

I need to stop this incessant chatter and work up an appetite for just *being*. Gently lured by the sea's distant roar, I begin to stroll to her music, tiptoeing over newly sprouted dune grass, trying not to destroy its work of holding together, via miles and miles of root, this very beach. Dune grass is admirably self-sufficient.

I remember a family picnic long ago on a similar remote beach, to which we carted babies, toys, bassinets, grills, food, everything needed to spend a day away together. We had only one son at the time, and he immersed himself in sand-castle building with assorted cousins and uncles, while my husband and I wandered off to make love in the dunes. The naughty danger of it created an unforgettable thrill. Sad to say, it was an isolated moment. Reaching adulthood before the Pill made me cautious, cool, not wild and free.

Before marriage I had played a kind of "sexual Russian roulette," doing everything except going all the way. This offered me the vicarious thrill of witnessing the man's pleasure, while my prize was the power of knowing I had contributed to his euphoria. Such safe sex or half sex kept me pure, but less than satisfied. Wild abandon was all but impossible on my wedding night. I couldn't suddenly let go just because some minister had sanctioned the once-forbidden act. I was trapped in a vicious cycle that led my husband eventually to label me frigid.

I'm walking faster now, through warm white sand, realizing even my feet are starved for stimulation. The entire island is sunning itself, and I am embracing its warmth. Although I cherish this time alone, I have a momentary craving to share it with a passionate lover. Instead, I receive a succulent substitute from the welcoming sea, its foam and crystals spewing high into the sky like a fountain, inviting me in to play.

A dark cloud obscures the sun, and I hug my shivers, running toward the water, not planning to plunge in, but doing so anyway. After the initial shock, I realize the water is warmer than the air and decide to stay in until the sun reappears. This is serious surf, though. I can't just drift. I must move with determination to ward off the undertow. *Never swim without someone watching from the shore* was always the rule; I'm breaking that one now, along with so many others. A gentle wave suddenly rises and towers overhead. Impulsively, I dive under, coming out the other side. I haven't dared that for years. In fact, I've had a phobia about going underwater for some time. Why am I more cautious as I age instead of the other way around? I wonder if it's all tied in to failure. I tend to forget my gains and remember only the losses. The failures have piled up, wreaking havoc with my confidence until, as an adult, I've become afraid to take chances.

Maddeningly, though, I watch my sons take risks. One has biked cross-country several times, and the other is a stand-up comic. They aren't afraid to fail, which they frequently do. I suppose I was just as bold at twenty: I got myself into drama school as the only undergraduate to do so, worked in the bush in Africa, became the secretary to the American ambassador's wife when I could hardly even type, talked my way into an editor's office to sell a magazine story without ever having been published before. Hell, I thought I was invincible for a long time, and then suddenly I stopped taking any risks. Inexplicably, there was a gradual erosion of faith in the essence of myself, as the habit of deference grew like a cancer on my soul until what I had become was out of my hands.

I think it was Picasso who said he spent the first half of his life becoming an adult and the last half learning to be a child. Is that why I have spent the last few summers gazing longingly at wide-eyed children? I was utterly entranced by one such child at the beach whose mother kept calling to her, "Victoria, do this . . . Victoria, do that." Victoria would have none of it; she was simply too immersed in her environment to eat or take a nap or be part of her family group. No, Victoria was in her own world—breaking all the rules, naked to the waist, hair caked with salt and sand—the embodiment of bliss.

I think I'm having some of that bliss right here and wish my kids could see me. They would applaud, no doubt, as I believe that our children want to see their parents happy, playful, even carefree. Once they gave me an Emerson quote about success, reading it aloud, flattering me by saying that it seemed to have been written about me. *"Successful people live well, laugh often, and love much. They've filled a niche and accomplished tasks so as to leave the world better than they found it, while looking for the best in others and giving the best they have."* "I'm working my way back to such success," I shout, as if the boys are watching from the shore, and gulp a mouthful of salt water.

I hear a snuffle, followed by a snort, and I dive under and swim into deeper water. The seals are here—not one, but many! Did they follow me from the other side? They must be trusting my presence now; in any case they are inspiring a momentary trust in myself. I dare to swim a bit closer as they pull at me like a magnet. I am under their spell and begin mimicking them, dipping in and up, rolling with the swells, then floating easily, the seals and me, suspended in time. Unexpectedly, a large breaker scoops me up, and I ride it on up to the beach, my thighs rubbing against the rushing sand granules. I am thrust ashore laughing—alone and laughing—lying spread-eagled, staring up at the vast sky, feeling delightfully foolish. Boy, have I ever allowed too many days to go dull and permitted too many parts of me to go unused. Perhaps in my next life I'll return as a seal and be forced to use all of me. Unless, of course, it's not too late for this life!

Just now I wish for a seal's extra coat of flesh. It's chilly, and I run up the beach for a towel and sweater, then huddle into a small hole of hollowed-out sand, wanting to stay with the seals and watch their antics. They are taking me by the hand and leading me back to my childhood, altering my sense of time, speaking to me with their bodies. One dives and reemerges with a large fish, which he devours while two others frolic aimlessly. They are masters at play, gazing back at me before taking each of their delicate, arching dives, as if to say, "This is what it's all about."

A concert of sounds engulfs me now—gulls honking, seals sniffling, waves spilling themselves farther and farther up onto the shore. It's a full-moon tide and should be higher than normal; maybe it will flood this entire spit of land. Will I be marooned, I wonder? I steady my nerves, knowing the moment of high tide is just that, a brief time that will always reverse itself and diminish. And so it is with me as I stand between my former life and the next stage. I rush to higher ground, trying to stay in the moment.

I envy how the seals handle their fat, furry bodies, instruments that truly work for them. Why am I not at home in my body? Probably because I am a large woman, and society only applauds the slight ones. What a waste to feel only shame and disgust for something that should be celebrated.

The loathing of my body started long ago, when I began turning chubby at nine or ten. My mother hid the snacks and tasty food and rationed my portions. I came to realize that my shape embarrassed her as we shopped for a winter coat and she refused to buy me the flashy aqua one I liked. "Not with *your* body," she said. "The camel-hair, double-breasted coat would suit you better."

In early adolescence I thinned out and was thrilled with my new circle skirt and pink sweater, which I tucked in to show off my waist. "What do you think?" I asked my father, pirouetting about the living room. "It's nice," he said, somewhat embarrassed, "except for that business on top."

My bulging breasts were the "business on top." Finally something acceptable was expanding, but in that moment I wished they, too, would shrink. My body image only worsened as I grew. Mothers in the fifties were determined to create finished products by the time their daughters were of marriageable age. Cut off from my body, I learned to play sophisticated games of flirtation, feigning submission in order to be more attractive.

My best friend told me that on her wedding day she felt like a piece of USDA Certified beef being led to slaughter. She had been inspected by doctors and dentists, then handed over to her groom like a prize animal.

Women's opinions of their bodies haven't changed that much. Emaciation is rampant. Starving is in! You can never be too rich or too thin. Not only do mothers push their daughters to be thin and beautiful, but they continue to push themselves, far into old age. No one seems as real or free as the seals in front of me. What a pity.

What attracts me to these adorable creatures most is their vulnerability and lack of constraint. Domestication seems to force women into such an unnatural state. Yet I eagerly and willingly played house throughout the sixties and seventies; the role of wife and mother was a virtuous endeavor. I baked bread, created healthy meals, orchestrated memorable parties; I was the perfect nurturer. I even slammed down the phone when I heard my husband's car pull into the driveway so I could greet him appropriately, matching his mood if it was good, perking him up if he was down.

Nobody asked me to behave in this fashion. It was more or less expected that a woman would create relationship first and herself second. It's beginning to occur to me that we got it all backward—that we need to attend to ourselves first. If I worried that my flight to the Cape was somehow narcissistic, I should abandon any such thoughts from here on out. Of primary importance now is for me to retrieve the buried parts of me—qualities like playfulness, vulnerability, being at home in my skin, using more of my instincts. Like so many pieces of a puzzle, I need to find a way to create the whole once again.

The tide rushes up like some unannounced visitor and washes over my feet, threatening to swallow me. I back away, rescuing my beach bag, and retreat to the sliver of dune, allowing every last sensation to sink into me.

I walk with clearer intent now, back to the place on the island where this adventure commenced, the great blue blur of ocean wavering behind. I'm recognizing happiness as it arrives.

Josh had promised to return at high tide, and sure enough, as the day wanes and the setting sun paints the sky orange, pink, and purple, his little boat rounds the point. I run to slip into my jeans, and wave him down. Wading out, I haul my body headfirst into the hull, now loaded with burlap bags bulging with freshly dug clams. Josh has harvested much, and so have I.

As we push off, the seals raise their heads to mark our departure. A few slide off the embankment and swim toward us, playing in the wake of our boat. But as we near town, they stop. Their soulful eyes meet mine one last time; they dive and swim away.

"So," Josh asks, "did you get what you wanted?"

I don't know what to say. How can I explain to this

practical man that I have spent the day swimming with seals? He may think I have lost my mind, as would half the other people in my life. I go for the easy answer. "What an incredible place," I say. "To think I've been summering here all these years and have never been out there."

He smiles and nods, as I shrink back into silence. A wave of melancholy sweeps over me, because I know such a day cannot be duplicated. So many compressed desires have been unleashed. I only hope I can nourish the resulting passion. I have found guidance through life's passages in books and lectures, but never before from a colony of animals.

In a very brief time, too brief, Josh is cutting the engines, and we are drifting into his slip. I gather my belongings and climb onto the dock as he unloads his clams and gives me a basketful of steamers and cherrystones. "You've worked up an appetite—enjoy 'em," he says.

"My favorite," I say. "You've given me so much today. Are you sure?"

"My pleasure."

I walk away, imagining a raw bar of cherrystones, salivating, and realize suddenly that I don't know how to open them; that's always been my husband's job. No time like the present.

It's a shock to be behind the wheel of a car, driving through a town, being part of its collective busyness. I am grateful to be heading home to my quiet place, tucked as it is in a scrub-pine forest a short way inland, at the end of a narrow, sandy path.

The cottage is cozy, womblike: beamed ceilings, seasoned wood that smells of salt air, kerosene lanterns I use more than electric lights. It is especially inviting after a day outdoors. I toss my wet clothes into the tub, put on some sweats, and take a bottle of wine from the refrigerator. I stop to gaze at a family picture, focusing on the fifty-year-old woman. I barely recognize her tight jaw, forced smile, eyelids drooping, hair streaked, more gray than blond.

They say you get the face you've earned by the time you're forty—all those sorrowful, angry expressions, long hidden behind makeup, become the naked truth. It mirrors who you are, who you've been, a kaleidoscope of endless patterns. Oh, well, for today at least I'm beginning to loosen up and like who I could be.

I uncork the wine and pour a glass. Settling into the window seat, I prepare to stare at a moonlit night. Today's adventure taught me how simple it is to be involved and uplifted by nothing more complicated than the unexpected. Me, the programmed woman with the low tolerance for boredom! I raise my glass to the future, just as the phone rings. Few have my number here. I consider letting it ring, but my curiosity gets the best of me. I dash for the receiver.

"Hi, it's me," my husband says. His hollow voice flattens my upbeat mood.

"Hi," I say tentatively. I've learned from several previous calls to listen hard and talk later. As the reality of our separation sinks in, he has become less friendly, more businesslike. The tenor of his voice tonight makes me uncomfortable.

"How are you doing?" he asks, a benign yet loaded question. If I say fine, and he is not fine, there will be hell to pay. I'm finding that unhappy people despise hearing good news from the contented ones. I stifle my impulse to tell him about my day, choosing to offer as little information as possible, waiting to hear the real agenda.

"The house sold," he announces matter-of-factly.

"Wow," I respond, realizing that as a couple we are now down to two homes—his and mine—with no old homestead to return to.

"We'll have some extra money," he continues. "I can rent a really nice place out here, and you can move in."

I pretend not to hear. He doesn't understand that I'm not interested in moving, period. Still, the wife in me feels obliged to offer something. "Perhaps I can visit some weekend," I reply, remaining as noncommittal as possible.

"Well, whatever," he says, backing off. Having made no specific arrangements when we parted, he probably thought after a couple of weeks I'd come to my senses and join him. The trouble is, I'm getting used to my solitude and, after a day like today, not only liking it but also seeing the worth of it.

It's not what he says that unnerves me but what he doesn't say. I have a habit of filling in blank spaces and make the grievous error of mentioning the seals.

"Seals," he says testily. "Where are they?"

"Monomoy."

"Who took you out there?"

"A fisherman friend."

"How did you meet *him?*"

No matter how I try to rescue the conversation, our moods begin to plunge. Now I'm feeling guilty and begin justifying my day, explaining more than I should. I feel strangely in his debt.

He allows that he would give anything to be wild and

free, "but one of us has to be practical, after all," he says. I stifle the urge to banter further, my spirit broken. The reality of my amazing day has dissolved, the comfort of my seclusion has been disturbed. How often have I allowed someone to spoil a perfectly good mood? I struggle to breathe as I hang up. Then, in a flash, I know why I'm here. I return to the pillow on the window seat and talk to the moon.

4

RIPTIDE

November

Woman must come of age by herself. She must find
her true center alone.

—*Anne Morrow Lindbergh,* GIFT FROM THE SEA

I've *taken* to chasing the light, which means rising when it is still dark and driving to the fish pier to view the fiery dawn. I'm always amazed to find others there, people who care to pay homage as one planet bows to the other, to see first a narrow pink stripe dividing water and sky, followed by a broad splash of pungent orange. As the sun now casts a glow on the faces nearby, I take a sip of coffee from my Thermos and inhale the crisp morning air.

It is one of those Cape Cod mornings when no sooner does the sun appear, bold and undaunted, than the clouds roll in. What was at first clear blue sky is suddenly dappled with fluffy pink clouds, which gradually become lavender and then a sullen gray, until the original picture dulls, as if someone has pulled a shade down to shut out the light. The Technicolor of dawn has lasted all of eight minutes, and now the sky is black and white. Fishermen are able to adjust to such mixed signals, checking the weather's subtle signs while preparing to launch their boats. Although the sky has changed, the sea remains calm, at least here in the harbor. It's different at the outer bar, where protected water meets open sea. Still, venturing out each day is a necessity for these men. They make their solitary decisions, sensing what's best for themselves and those they leave behind. Overcast skies don't call for them to scrap their day—they just proceed with more caution, taking nothing for granted. So it should be with each of us as we begin a new day.

I'm reminded of a hot August afternoon a few years back, when my husband and I took a picnic to the outer bar. The surf was inviting and the sun brutal, so we kept dipping in and out of the refreshing water. On the last dip we became more aggressive, swimming farther away from shore, unaware at first that a riptide was pulling us apart. No matter how hard we tried to swim together, we seemed stuck in independent courses. As wave after gigantic wave began crashing down, it became clear that getting back to safety would be an entirely individual issue. We each would have to swim for it or drown.

The same seems remarkably true of our lives now. Having drifted off course, we have no choice but to find our way back, with or without each other. There are no lifeguards, no inner tubes to save us—inner strength and *will* our only lifelines. I watch now as the fishermen maneuver their boats slowly, carefully, in and around buoys as if on some slalom course. It is a craft, an art form, just to get out of the harbor, but the distant roar of the sea beckons, and they seem driven to follow. Some go it alone, but most venture out with a crew, each possessing a well-developed skill that will serve him best when all the men pool resources and work in tandem. Such is the way to land a sizable catch. Such is also the way to lead a successful life.

If only my husband and I had learned to work more in concert! I sensed a need for a deeper sharing from the beginning. Perhaps our Peace Corps life in Africa worked well because we had to depend on one another for virtually everything. Certainly our son and his wife, on their biking tours, are establishing a bond stronger than most of their peers possess. Yet many of us entered marriage as only half a person, expecting to be completed by the other. We held dear to the fantasy that the man waiting at the end of the aisle had all the answers.

Once, when my husband and I had a disagreement, he blurted out, "We're not making it, sweetie." The truth of those words terrified me, and I quickly denied them, redoubling my efforts to make right whatever was wrong. Those were the days when the children were young and the stakes were high—becoming a single mother was unthinkable. Underneath I harbored doubts. Underneath was where I had been trained to keep them. I was obsessed with relationship and held high my illusion of what marriage should be. Perhaps now I grieve the death not of my marriage but simply the illusion of marriage.

It has grown cold and drizzly. Most of the boats have cleared the harbor. I wish I were out there with them, with some goal for the day. Being alone doesn't come easily to someone who has always liked inclusion. Stepping outside marriage is as difficult as not coming to the rescue of a needy child. It has taken more than a month to understand what I've done—what I still need to do.

But every time I replay the phone call of the other night I feel relieved, even privileged, to be apart from those who have for so long looked to me to make everything work, to be without duty or schedule. Instead I stand here and dream and wonder and watch as the sea empties and fills itself up again.

Just now I'm among a collage of people all of whom seem to be in varying degrees of seeking. I wonder about my fellow dawn-worshippers, imagining their lives to be more interesting than mine. Whatever my life lacks, I fantasize these strangers already have—wild sex, cozy evenings beside a hearth, perfect jobs, capable children. However, while such visions initially entertain me, they soon depress me, until I remind myself of all the clandestine chats I've had with friends who tattle on their truth and tell their secrets—women who've been made to have too much sex, or who never have sex, or who have put on naughty black nighties and played "dirty" to enliven a man, or participated in a ménage à trois, or are victims of passive aggression, or must endure someone who cheats, or someone who is simply dull.

Still, it's hard now to watch the passion of two young lovers leaning against a nearby pickup truck, enveloped in a blanket and each other, or the hard-bodied jogger running to stay fit for what I imagine must be some equally gorgeous partner, or a couple ensconced in a Mercedes, not talking, just being together at peace.

I'm overcome with envy and momentarily wish to be held, until I'm distracted by a middle-aged couple. He's staring straight ahead, stone-faced, hands stuffed into his parka pockets, alone with his thoughts. His wife has wandered off, hiding her face under a hood, equally alone, estranged. I remember an evening with my husband, years ago. We had escaped to a romantic inn in hopes of refueling our sagging spirits. There we sat, in a picture-perfect setting, sharing a bottle of Pinot Noir. My husband turned the spotlight on me. Flattered to be asked about my reading and research at that time, which involved sensuality and sexuality, I waxed poetic about the meaning of eroticism. There was a method to my madness. I hoped he might catch on and we would proceed in kind. But what ensued was a debate. I heard a man hungry for sex and fed up with a woman who lived too much in her head. I became quiet, and he became stony. A curtain came down between us.

For now I must take solace in watching the solitary walkers as they pass, mostly middle-aged women like me. Their faces display a determined power and seem free of encumbrances, no longer stranded in others' lives. Their strides suggest confidence and self-respect; they are relieved, perhaps, to be away from the turmoil of relationship. I suffer less pain alone, it seems, than in the presence of an indifferent partner.

Still, there's a price to pay for such self-indulgence. I stand here holding freedom in one hand and guilt in the other—guilt not only for failing my husband, somehow, but for having hidden thoughts that do not include him. I felt compelled to make sure we were roughly similar and worked hard to bridge every gap. Our differences frightened me. Surely they were signs on my part of some vague infidelity. Even now leaving him seems to have been a grievous sin—a silly attempt at belated adolescence. The critic in my personality continues to blame me for stepping outside the norm. Why should I be allowed to indulge myself in such wild abandon when he cannot do the same?

Poor fellow! He comes from that generation of men who counted on wives to be wives, who needed a wife not only to take care of things but for the sake of respectability. It doesn't look good for us to be living apart. My sense is that only if we get back together and restore our life will he stop being angry.

And so I wonder how long I can extend this separation and hold the guilt at bay while I repair and revive. I remember the words of a friend who insisted, at a dinner party no less, that anyone who claims to be in love all the time is a liar. "I have been blissfully happy for five or six years," she announced, "felt tolerable in the relationship for ten, was semi-miserable for four, and mildly contented the rest of the time." I marveled at her honesty, considering that her husband sat beside her. But I, too, have come to appreciate that I can't fake what I don't feel, and that too much vitality is used up trying.

Doesn't change occur only when we stop living the expected life? For sure, marriage, like any other institution, cannot contain and should not restrain anyone. Hell, every marriage needs community relief. How could one partner, no matter how remarkable, be everything to the other? It's ludicrous to believe so. I've no choice now but to fall in love as soon as possible—not with a man but with my immediate life and eventually myself. I'm free to make my own decisions and equally free to take the consequences. For once to be harsh, indifferent, unfeeling is liberating. At the very least, being so permits me to cultivate the other half of my whole. So I've declared my freedom and am somewhat at peace with it. What's left is to make sure there's no residual guilt.

It is eight in the morning, and the day is in full swing.

Action surrounds me. I am awake to my immediate reality: I need a job, not only to augment my savings but to save my sanity. Asking my husband to meet even my slightest financial need seems preposterous. I want to pay for my own lipstick, underwear, and entertainment; I don't want to feel beholden. Before me in the window of Nickerson's Fish Market is a HELP WANTED sign. I head for the door and walk in without a moment's hesitation. The owner is busy cutting fish on a marble slab. He peers up at me over his half-frames, as the doorbell jingles.

"May I help you?" he inquires, expecting me to buy fish, I suppose, not ask for a job. Strong men in yellow rubber aprons are in the backroom hauling giant boxes of fish packed in ice; there is not a woman in sight. What kind of a job could there be for the likes of me, I wonder?

"I need . . . I mean, wish to apply for the job advertised in the window," I blurt out.

"You want to work here?" he asks, chuckling at such an idea. I'm middle-aged and not even officially local. The fish pier is staffed almost entirely with locals. "Why would you want to work here?" he asks.

"I love the waterfront," I say, and then add without thinking, "I'm a writer always in search of a story." The words again areout of my mouth before they are formed.

He puts his knife down, wipes his hands on a rag, and comes closer, peering at me behind his glasses. "It's tough work, y'know—hauling and weighing fish, climbing up to the lobster tanks, dealing with the customers."

"I'm up to it," I lie. "Besides, don't you close at Christmas for the winter? If I don't work out, you can get rid of me then, without any hard feelings."

"I suppose you're right," he says. "How bout reporting for work in the morning?"

And so I become part of the job force. I have found a lifeline, for now.

5

WATER THERAPY

Late November

*We cannot write in water . . . we cannot carve in water. Water's
nature is to flow and that is how we should
treat life . . . emotion, negative or positive. Do not deny it
but always let it flow through and then away.*

—*Anonymous*

Driving *to* work under cement skies makes my arrival there all the more heartwarming. The fish market itself is ablaze in light, everything inside painted a white enamel that shimmers on even the darkest days. The trip is brief and uneventful, along winding country roads until I reach the sea and weave along the shoreline for a few more miles. Today it is bitter cold, with a wind from the northeast stirring up ruffles of whitecaps that decorate the surface of the water as far as I can see. The ocean is charged with energy, which in turn charges me. As I enter the market, the side door is seized by the wind and slams shut behind me. The backroom is bustling as the floor is littered with freshly caught cod, sole, and halibut, waiting to be filleted. I tiptoe over the fish bodies, their fixed eyes staring up at me, hang my coat on a hook, and report to the front, where several customers are waiting.

"May I help you?" I ask two men who seem mesmerized by something in the lobster pool.

"We're wondering if you have a dead lobster in there," one of them replies. I peer down. A two-pounder is huddled in a corner, isolated, totally still. On closer observation, I detect a subtle undulation—its shell appears to be hovering slightly above the body.

"It's molting," the owner says nonchalantly, "shedding one skin to grow more flesh and become larger."

"Amazing," I whisper, still staring. It occurs to me that you don't often get to witness growth and change. I respect the instincts of a molting lobster, hiding out while it is raw and vulnerable until it becomes tough and resilient once again.

Working in and around water, with its gushing, splashing, and slurping sounds, transforms an otherwise mundane job into a sensuous experience. It's like water play. Being here day after day is beginning to relieve my spiritual drought, the routine of work staving off depression, reinvigorating me.

I'm into my third week, and there is still the sense of novelty. The very mention of where I work raises eyebrows. I'm amused by people's reactions. "You're doing what?" a neighbor asks. She thinks the fish business is men's work. I get a kick out of proving myself—hauling and weighing buckets of lobster, shucking scallops and clams for chowder base—all the while knowing that the men in the backroom, no less than my neighbor, are looking me up and down and wondering where the hell I've come from.

What no one knows, and I had forgotten, is that I've been drawn to this place for years. This ramshackle shed, which sits on the water's edge and hasn't changed for as long as I can remember, is a comfort to me. In past years I'd watch fishwives shuck scallops on the dock while others baited hooks and mended nets nearby, but I could never have guessed that I would one day be doing similar things. Being the opposite of what I was before is opening up new vistas.

Even so, there are drawbacks. The dress code, for one— jeans or khaki pants, with a tucked-in navy-blue top. Never having had a decent waist, I usually hide my figure in oversized baggy sweaters. I hold on to my vanity, however, by donning the yellow plastic bib apron worn mostly by the men. Then there's the temperamental cash register that beeps and buzzes whenever I hit the wrong key, which happens to be several times a day. The noise heralds the owner's wife, who sighs at my stupidity as she voids my error, while the impatient customers watch and wait. I then begin these transactions all over again, feeling as embarrassed and stupid as I did back in college, when I'd take on part-time jobs that were over my head and end up failing or getting fired.

When, if ever, will I get it? Still, I remain the good sport, trying to cover up my insecurity by being more eager and enthusiastic, even though my flushed cheeks and perspiring face suggest shame and distress.

I try not to take myself or the work too seriously, but I do have utility and other bills to pay. I'm addicted to perfection and need to please, but more often feel as though I disappoint. Too proud and needy to quit, I make up for my inadequacies by arriving early and leaving late, not taking pay for the extra hour or so I work. Why is it I always feel that when someone hires me, they are doing me a service instead of the other way around? How quickly I'm reduced to feeling like a child, craving praise and appreciation, needing reassurance about my performance. My father used to tell me I was supersensitive. Well, who likes to be found wrong all the time? Who enjoys criticism?

I've always wanted to be like my brilliant older brother, who stood by the phone one April day in his senior year of high school taking call after call from Ivy League colleges offering him assorted scholarships and awards. When my turn came, a guidance counselor told my concerned mother where nonachievers such as myself were being accepted. I was sent off to a junior college—a finishing school, as they were called back then—intended for attractive, dumb blondes to be groomed and polished and sent out, not to a bigger world but to the confines of marriage. The trouble was, the school fell short of finishing me. Instead, it left gaps in my heart and soul that I am now trying to fill.

My ego is what is really being tamed in this job. It's taking some getting used to being a servant, not a master. The Yankee natives give me orders without looking me in the eye, or they insist on being served by the proprietor, who they are certain will give them special favors. At first I was insulted by these people of means. I'm of value, too! Like them, I've traveled the world, been educated, even written a couple of books. But who cares what they think? What I'm trying to do here is not about impressions. Instead, I mind my own business, speak when I'm spoken to, cut their fish, and pretend to like serving them.

My only pretense involves the owner's wife, who thinks I'm a happily married quasi-bohemian, hanging around the waterfront in order to write a book. If she only knew. But I'm not going to confess my ambiguous marital state to her, especially since she and her husband seem a close-knit team, equally dependent, one with the other. Besides, I'm fast becoming aware that married women don't much trust unmarried ones. She and I banter back and forth, mostly about husbands and children, when she's not listening to customers' tales of woe. The market is a veritable town hall. People don't come in here just to buy fish; they seek affirmation and come to pass news. We always know who is getting married and who is getting buried.

Seeing the same faces day after day, I can just about guess the truth of their lives. There are the widows on fixed incomes who come for just a few ounces of cod, and the working-class wives, young mothers, who want to buy swordfish but can afford only catfish. There are those that ask for fish heads and lobster bodies, claiming they want them for bait; I figure they're making chowder they will need to stretch for two meals. There are the wealthy ones, "kept women" I call them, who live in rambling oceanfront homes with wicker furniture on the porch, flowers delivered weekly, expensive casual clothes from Neiman Marcus, who bask in soaking tubs and use bidets and order whole fillets of salmon, instructing me as they breeze out the door, "Put it on the tab."

I've never had the privilege of being "kept," if, in fact, it is a privilege. I look at the scrupulously scrubbed faces of these mannequinlike women and wonder, Does having it all make you happier or sadder? Does it make you free?

My back is aching, but several lobster tanks need to be scrubbed. I think I'm more than a tad bit jealous of them. Still, there are ground rules I'm certain they must live by, rules set up by their husbands and society that they must obey. Earning one's own keep has a great deal of merit.

I remind myself each time I want to quit that this job is about my independence as well as learning to rise above criticism, honor my ignorance, and deal with my occasional arrogance. And, having surrendered to a simpler life, I am finding excitement in little things that others might think dull.

Tonight it's about hanging out. I wasn't looking forward to an entire evening alone. One of the guys in the back stops me at the door. "Want a beer?" he asks as he does every night.

"You know I don't drink beer," I answer. "Now, if you were offering wine . . ."

"As a matter of fact I am," he says, lifting the lid on the ice chest and producing a bottle of Gallo Chablis. Not my brand, but the invitation to stay awhile seems delicious. Besides, I'm a sucker for anyone who presupposes a wish or need. Hungry for connection, I dare to dally, throwing my coat aside and sitting down on the nearest overturned bucket. There's no need to hold myself aloof anymore. These guys are all the community I have right now.

The unpretentious wine is as refreshing as the conversation, sprinkled with off-color remarks and jokes. I'm laughing, something I haven't done for weeks. Laughter requires company, unless, of course you're laughing at yourself! It feels good to linger—not to be running home or racing off to an obligation. Of course, I have none of those here, not as in my former life, which was driven by the calendar. I'm relishing these weathered men of thirty who look forty, who make time for one another and value their camaraderie.

I gulp one glass, then another. They wonder about my family, my life alone, but hesitate to ask too much. Fishermen are loners. They keep to themselves and accord the same privilege to others. I sense they like me, even respect how well

I work. I love being the voyeur, seeing behind the scenes, knowing more about unknown lives. Sitting here with these young men makes me miss my boys. I wonder what they're up to, wish we could hang out together like this. These guys have no idea how much their letting me in delights me. I feel a part of something. For now, I'm one of them.

6

WAVES OF TRUTH

Late December

To arrive where you are, to get there from where you are not, You must go by a way wherein there is no ecstasy.

—*T.S. Eliot, "East Coker"* FOUR QUARTETS

The chill of the house awakens me each morning, and I hustle to put another log on the wood-burning stove before the red-hot coals turn to ash, after which I place a kettle of water on top of the same stove and sit huddled nearby to wait for its whistle.

Such is my morning ritual, nothing terribly complicated unless I've forgotten to bring logs in from the woodpile the night before. I'm deep into my time-out season of life, where it seems best to be actively passive, involved in little, aware of much. Instinct told me to take myself away and look at all the unwrapped gifts nature has to offer. The natural world is hibernating, and so am I.

In former years, winter days and nights meant hunkering down, gathering in, the fireplace crackling, chili bubbling on the stove, and the boys sweaty and energized from basketball games, filling the house with the magic of their youth. Now I'm down to dinner for one, conversations with myself, hauling and chopping wood, and continuing on my private pilgrimage as I grapple with darkness, in hopes of seeing the light. This remote peninsula, extending into the sea, makes it easier for the pilgrim to stay true to her quest even at this most festive time of year, because here the spirit of the season is contained somehow.

I've always loved the intention of Christmas, but lately

I've been overwhelmed by its excessiveness. When I see the exhausted expressions on women's faces as they run around trying to please, I realize that modern-day Christmas seems to happen at the expense of women. We have taken on the job of infusing our homes with joy, whether the family wants it or not. In past years I was so consumed by this imperative that I staged a holiday party for twenty or so families, complete with crafts, carols, and buffet dinner, importing people and their accompanying merriment to ensure that we would be full of joy.

And even if I had been a woman who entertained effortlessly (which I'm not), I was always the last to catch the spirit, so caught up was I in creating it for everyone else. My old book club always ended up canceling the December meeting. "We've no time," the women would say, "no time to meet, much less read." What a pity, I thought. Surely the producers of Christmas needed time off more than anyone. A few of us did manage an evening last year. We sipped sherry and shared Christmas memories. It turned out to be the most magical night of the season.

I'm glad I have that simple memory to recall just now, as I'm shunning anything seasonal, instead gliding solo like a skater from one part of the pond to the other, a stark contrast from the usual holiday clutter.

This is definitely not the year for engraved cards or Christmas letters. I've received few and am sending none, letting the answering machine hold both wishes and questions at bay. Since I'm still unclear as to my future, I've come to hate inquiries that make me produce logical answers. In place of talk, I record ideas in my journal, then cling to the thought, "To live is to change, and to strive toward a more perfect life is to have changed often." But really, do I have to go to such extremes?

I decide to leave for work early today in order to stop at a tiny chapel I've been frequenting. It is nestled in a hollow of pine trees at the end of town, and once inside, I take to my knees in the darkened sanctuary, asking whomever will listen to forgive me for such things as leaving my husband, wanting more than I deserve, and choosing a course of action that continues to seem narcissistic.

Churches have a humbling effect on me—sometimes they even stabilize me. I wouldn't think of trying to sell a story or a book without first stepping into a church on the way to a meeting with editors. Today I seem to want to just sit and absorb any message the spirits care to bestow upon me. I become haunted by the empty crèche that sits on the altar waiting to be filled with the Holy Family and their visitors. By leaving my home and husband, have I emptied our personal crèche for good? I hope not, but the trouble with Christmas is that it brings such reminders and triggers such questions.

I take my leave, feeling troubled instead of calm, and hope that the drive through town will brighten me up. There are wreaths adorning gray shingles, electric candles lighting up windowsills, and a hardware store bursting with shiny red wagons and Flexible Flyer sleds. Fortunately this quiet enclave lacks most of the glitz and glitter that never fail to depress me. I'm able to avoid the psychic bombardment. Still, I can't shield myself from seasonal nostalgia each time a customer at the fish market places a large order. You can tell by how many pounds of lobster and oysters they order, just how many people they're entertaining and when the family will arrive. A melancholia overtakes me as I realize that my boys won't be home. I was such a good sport when they told me about their Christmas plans that did not include us, but secretly I felt abandoned. Not wanting to appear pushy, I accepted their decisions and hoped they would be home next year. I knew that after they were married we'd have to share their time, but knowing it and experiencing it are different things. We haven't enjoyed this holiday as a family for three years. The rituals just seemed to stop, like all the other natural endings—such as the last time one of the boys crawled into bed with us, or I carried them on my hip, or saw them naked, even. Such moments evaporate so quietly that you don't realize it's the last time until long afterward. I envy divorced people who are forced to divvy up time with the kids and are made to stick with it.

Just now the fish-market radio is playing "I'll Be Home for Christmas," and I am overcome enough to duck into the bathroom and have a good cry. My husband will be coming, which makes me all the more teary. Are we up for a reunion just yet? I don't know, but the alternative of each of us being alone seemed unthinkable. Tears come easily when I'm needy. I dab my eyes, gulp my grief, and head back toward the customers, where I spot a white-bearded man wearing a hand-knitted stocking cap. He's peering at me through metal-frame glasses. "You must be Santa Claus!" I say, forcing a cheery greeting.

"Been called that," he answers.

"I bet you've played him, too," I say.

"Just yesterday," he says with a twinkle.

"Well, I've been naughty *and* nice," I continue, enjoying the charade. "Know what I want for Christmas?"

"You have everything you want," he says, not missing a beat, and with that, exits the store.

What was that all about? I wonder, momentarily dumbfounded. What does he know about me? How could he possibly claim that I have everything I want? I am agitated, testy even, and I don't know why. It must look to people that I have everything—good health, creative career, time away, solid kids, a loyal husband. What else is there?

Plenty, I think as I sling a tray of filleted cod into the ice case. I want to be happy, that's for starters, to feel again and not just be numb, to laugh more and have someone to cry with. The nerve of that Santa character, laying such a trip on me. I suddenly have this gagging sensation that says I have everything I was *told I should want,* but that's a far cry from what I really desire! It's hard for most of the women I know to state what they want, because they've gotten used to wanting only what's available.

At least I'm beginning to see what *I no longer want:* things like making life pleasant for others while forgoing my own desires, writing the script for the last act of our marriage without my husband's participation. I don't want to have to deal with my partner's bad moods, his stony silences, wondering if they have anything to do with me while my own spontaneity is squashed.

Still, I hate myself for never being satisfied. I should be more grateful and accept the status quo, but obviously I wouldn't be here if I could. Perhaps the encounter with Santa was fortuitous. It's high time I ask myself the tough questions before my husband arrives with questions of his own.

A blizzard is brewing, and the market is closing early. "You'd best be on your way," the owner warns, knowing I don't have four-wheel drive. "Don't forget our Christmas party, Friday night," he adds. "It will be a last hurrah before we batten down the hatches 'til Memorial Day." A party! The last thing I want to do is make an appearance alone, socializing with people I barely know. What will I wear? I've left all my good clothes in storage. I'll check the minute I get home, I say to myself, making a quick exit into the blustery wind, pulling my jacket collar up as high as it will go and huddling in its warmth.

As the lights of the village drop behind me, I am momentarily lost, like the astronauts during the blackout period when they're returning to the earth's atmosphere. The snow is blowing across the empty road. I shift into second gear and creep. The noise of ice chunks scraping against my windshield wipers creates a sort of eerie music. I can barely see in front of me, yet I can see everything. I am inside a glass ball, those Christmas toys that children shake. Being in the storm is scary but invigorating. I just manage to find my own driveway through the whirling snow, and savor the relief when I'm finally home.

Once inside, I slam the door, bolt it as if to shut out the world. A cup of cocoa and a newly stoked fire will be my tonic for the moment. I will sit with my journal and just be, yet even in the silence my mind chatters on. I ponder that most-asked question of the season: What do you want? We usually answer with some material object. Imagine if we said something like a better state of mind, or togetherness, or simply to be surrounded by laughter. Last year my son asked for my Christmas list over the phone. I promptly responded by saying, "A tape of you singing holiday music." He laughed at my request, but it was my real desire, to hear his voice as smooth as maple syrup, the sound more soothing for me than an aria by the Three Tenors.

C. S. Lewis spoke of something he called "felt satisfaction," which he interpreted as "a quality of fullness . . . an immediacy worth perpetuating." I try to imagine what that might be. Sitting here alone is satisfying enough, but the night would be far better if shared with another—with someone whose mood meets mine, who relishes moments, whose wonder remains untainted, who appreciates simple things and says so, who laughs much, indulges heartily, is spontaneous in spirit, is quick to embrace, and sees joy as a duty!

Oh, dear, now I've gone too far. Who could ever be that way? Still, just a few of these qualities would be enough. Isn't this what's missing in my marriage? I am astonished that my wants are attainable. What's more, they don't take money or power, just a little attitude change. So why isn't this within my grasp?

Aha, because grasping isn't the way—reaching perhaps, but not being overt about it. That's how I've failed in the past, wanting others to be a certain way and trying to push and cajole them in that direction. Good things seem just to happen along. The state of feeling satisfied occurs most often when I haven't sought it. If only I can break with fixed notions, I might see new possibilities in relationship.

I'm beginning to grasp some idea of what I want. For starters, I want to take no action, "pursue that which is not meddlesome," says the Chinese philosopher Lao Tzu. Having taken myself away, I am in a frame of mind to wait and see rather than manipulate and direct. Living with nature has taught me the dignity of being without motive. Occupying this tiny cottage with no clutter, only barren essentials, has served to help me find more in less.

Speaking of less, I need to find some decent party clothes. My all-but-empty closet looks bleak. There's a green velour pantsuit, several pairs of khakis and blue jeans, a tweed blazer, plaid culottes, and, hidden under a plastic bag fresh from the cleaners, my black crepe pantsuit, which I've all but forgotten I owned. Perfect, I think, stripping down to my underwear and stepping into the pants, only to find them impossible to button. Damn! I wasn't aware I had gained weight, but living under layers and eating whatever I pleased has obviously added some unwanted fat. Panicked now that nothing will fit, I begin grabbing at tops and bottoms, mixing and matching in an effort to put something together, experiencing several hot flashes in the process. Up till now it hasn't mattered how I dressed, and I don't like suddenly worrying about it. Mercifully, the velour pants with the elastic waist work well with a black cowl-neck sweater. A little jewelry and I'll be presentable. Phew! Now back to the quiet business of the season.

My grandmother used to say, "As the hands toil, so the spirit is raised above the troubled motions of the mind." There's stollen to make, mince pies, Newburg sauce, and butter cookies. What would December be without the smell of cinnamon, nutmeg, and cloves? I reach for a saucepan, pour in some aging cider, add the nostalgic spices, and let it bubble away on the stove to create the aroma I've been craving.

Next I put Pavarotti's Christmas CD on the stereo, open a bottle of wine, and choose happiness over righteousness for now. Being right almost always ends in splendid isolation anyway. 'Tis the season to put the past away—I'm feeling a bit like the recovered Scrooge—new and happy and grateful for a few waves of truth.

7

Silent Seas, Silent Nights

Christmas

For a few days, once a year, the atrophied souls of grown-ups are filled again with that spirit which inspires the wisdom of fools and children.

—*Michael Harrison*, THE STORY OF CHRISTMAS

I*t is* the day before the day before Christmas. He'll be here in a few hours. I've nailed a homemade wreath onto a tree at the end of the lane and will light the kerosene lanterns and candles before he arrives. I am nervous, afraid that I will revert back to the wife role just when I'm getting used to being happily single. I've prepared all our traditional food in an absolute orgy of domestication, to please our palates as well as to soothe our souls. Soul food for Christmas—I like the sound of it. Figuring we get to experience only seventy or eighty Christmases in a lifetime, I am determined to enjoy this one my way, no matter who is or isn't around. I read somewhere that the Frenchwoman's role is to please others, but to please herself in the process! This concept is new for me, that my own joy is my responsibility. Only I can receive it, and, likewise, only I can allow others to take it away. Not this Christmas! I've had my fill of bleak midwinters and now set my sights on joy.

I hear his car, see the headlights through windowpanes etched in frost. I throw on my coat, toss a scarf around my neck, and head out to greet him. For three months I've been testing aloneness. Now I face awkward togetherness. This is real life moving right along and high adventure as well—Christmas and the two of us, alone!

There is a tentative embrace that unnerves me, and so I

grab his suitcase and hurry back inside, reminding myself that he has had a long drive and hasn't spent these last few months pondering as I have—or has he? How has his bachelor life taken shape? He's been a loner most of his life. I wonder if he is enjoying his solitude all the more. I will refrain from asking questions just now and let the evening develop its own rhythm.

It has been his habit to inspect every inch of the cottage each time he arrives, and tonight is no exception. I fix him a scotch, which he carries with him from room to room. Once he learns that all is well in his lair, he settles into a rocking chair and places his long legs on a stool in front. I sit on the couch, legs curled under me. He sighs, sips his drink, and seems mildly content. I'm frankly petrified, empty of agenda, so I wait to see what transpires. It will take some time, I fear, to locate the tender and live spots in each other. He has grayed considerably since the fall, and his face looks weathered and drawn. I wonder how I appear to him? Do I look rested and bright-eyed or tense, like the day we parted? Stingy as he is with both compliments and criticisms, I'll probably never find out.

His drink disappears too fast, and I offer to refill it. "Please," he says, as I walk briskly for the ice, leaving the weight of silence behind. Silence is a good friend, I repeat, as if saying a mantra. It allows for the natural progression of things. Still, I remain nervous, anxious to fill the void as I used to with the interesting questions, chitchat, sweet nothings that nice girls like me were taught to utter. I sure did have that nice-girl persona down pat. Now, what takes the place of nice, I wonder?

"How are you?" I ask. "I mean really."

"Things are okay," he says blandly. "I've joined a health club, playing some indoor tennis, trying to reduce this." He points to his portly middle. "It's all those TV dinners."

I feel a pang of guilt; he's touched the mother in me. I suddenly want to cook for him, send him back to his place with a cooler full of casseroles.

"You'll have to come down some weekend. You'd like my place," he continues, teasing me with a description. "It's an old barn that looks like Ralph Lauren designed it."

"Maybe next month," I answer, wanting to offer some gesture of goodwill, "now that I'm finished at the fish market."

"The fish market," he says. "Joan the fishmonger!" He's lighthearted in his sarcasm, actually fascinated. "What did you do there?" he wonders, and asks more, as if he's really intrigued about the fishermen, the waterfront, everything. We are on our best behavior, yet it doesn't feel artificial or contrived. I'm thinking how pleasant it is when two people try to be gentle with one another.

"Would you like another glass of wine?" he asks, noticing that my glass is empty. I nod, and he goes off to fetch the bottle. My mind wanders to a friend who trained monks in ritualization. "When they started Communion," she explained, "they would pick up the chalice without giving it any thought, purely an object to be used, not treated as holy. What they needed to learn was the importance of developing a relationship with liturgical things and become involved with them. Only then would the ceremony have meaning." Listening to her, I couldn't help but imagine what my world might be like if I looked at the human beings I was closest to as holy and treated them with that same sense of respect. These thoughts flash through my mind as he returns. I try to look deeper into his heart, at the human being behind the roles of husband, father, educator. Seeing him apart from mortal agendas permits a sort of genuineness of spirit to float about the room. Whatever toughness he brought home with him seems to be melting away. Perhaps we'll be able to find some neutral ground.

After soup and bread I suggest a game of cards. He says he's tired, ready for bed. I feel my first pang of rejection. Tired, to me, has always been synonymous with boredom. Still, I agree, it's late. I blow out the candles and head for the loft, wondering if we'll fall into the same bed. He gives me a peck on the cheek and heads for the guest room. Wind howls outside our thin walls. I wonder about sex, even though I'm not at all sure I'm interested. Is there another woman? Is he in contact with his college sweetheart, who constantly keeps in touch with us, or the woman to whom he sent flowers last year, the bill inadvertently coming to me. I sigh and go into what has become my own room, pushing away such thoughts. This has been an eventful evening, an evening that had the potential to be hard but was soft. Perhaps a Christmas is in the making.

He is up long before I am. I can hear the scrape of the shovel as he attempts to dig us out of several inches of snow. The aroma of coffee permeates the house, and for the first time in months I don't have to make it myself. He's left me a cup on the bedside table, an old habit. I had forgotten what a treat that was. The house is toasty. I can hear the logs crackling in the stove and linger in bed a while longer before dressing and going downstairs. He's still outside, so I knock on the window and mouth a good morning.

It's overcast but no longer snowing. I prepare a breakfast of bacon and eggs. Over a second cup of coffee, I say, "Want to go to the beach?"

He stares. "You've got to be kidding."

"No, I mean it. I've never been to the beach after a snowstorm. It would be an adventure!" At the beginning of our marriage he was always quoting a line from *The Matchmaker* about the importance of having adventures.

"Hell, why not," he says, surprising me.

Within minutes we are in the car, skidding down our icy road. I can't believe it. He hates the cold, frequents the beach only in the best of circumstances. Perhaps this gesture is an olive branch—maybe he's ripe for anything—perhaps the gambler in him doesn't want to let the dare go by. No matter, we're outside, and somehow nature always seems to generate unity.

I hold the wheel tightly. Once at the beach, on the narrow track that cuts through the dunes, we head out toward the edge of my world. Some say the next stop is Portugal! I'm certain he thinks I've lost my mind as I drive onto the semihard sand. He says as much: "What if we get stuck?"

"I do this often," I say. "We've had freezing weather for the past week—we should be fine." Still, I sense his uneasiness. As usual, I'm the one who wants to throw caution to the wind while he plays it safe. We are ensconced in a white world, snowy heaps upon snowy heaps blown smooth, scalloping the dunes as if with marshmallow topping. I exclaim about the majesty, hoping to initiate a response from him, some welcome affirmation.

"Shall we stop here?" I ask.

"It's your call," he answers, absolving himself of responsibility. We stop at a spot wide enough for me to turn back around. "C'mon," I say, eager to get out and explore. All is quiet, eerily so, a dead-end world, yet bright and beautiful. I walk ahead, coaxing him toward the top of a dune. In front of us lies Nantucket Sound, appearing like an open field, a seascape frozen in place with icy strips decorating its surface, looking like whitecaps on a restless summer sea. I've never seen it like this, a normally restless body of water now a silent picture, a still life—the ocean seeming still and frozen, like our marriage. The danger, I think, lies in refusing to admit to being frozen, keeping dissatisfaction a secret, so that one day you end up sitting in the middle of a frozen surface not knowing when the ice will crack and thaw.

I can tell he's less moved. He has a detached look that tells me his thoughts are elsewhere, not here with me. I take his arm and nudge him closer to shore. We are amazed to find that all is not still. Thick sheets of ice move gently to the rhythm of the tides, a subtle undulation. This slow-motion sea, usually roaring, is now whispering. I hear a quiet splash from somewhere under the glacial surface that sounds like the rustling of a taffeta skirt. Then I spot a seal, not swimming, but sitting upright on a raft of ice, drifting at the whim of the waters. "Can you see him?" I say, pointing with one hand, squeezing my husband's arm with the other. He shakes his head in wonder. A broad smile spreads across his face. For one brief moment we seem kindred spirits. Then a burst of arctic air and a sudden snow squall interrupt our momentary enchantment. "I'm heading back," he says. "Take your time. I know this is your thing." He disappears into the flurry of snowflakes, looking to me like a phantom on a spatter-painted postcard.

Turning back to the sea, I notice two boats and a dinghy iced in. They will remain so until the thaw. Their owners can no more loosen them from the grip of ice than I can unthaw our marriage. I'm reminded to simply stay *in* the season and stop trying to play God. In time the tide will turn, and thawing weather will replace the arctic chill. I start back to the car, thinking there is much to garner from frozen flats and icy seas.

A veil of snow blocks all that is beyond me. Shy, unsure, I put one foot in front of the other, not unlike our wedding day when he was waiting for me at the front of the altar, then smiling and tearful. Now he is disguised behind a steamed-up car window and a blanket of snow. The image is as blurred as our future. I am suddenly wistful and weary, but nevertheless I take time for one last indulgence, making an angel in the snow, flapping my arms and legs while staring up at the white sky, pausing for just a moment in hopes of hearing the angels speak.

"What are you doing, you crazy lady?" he calls from the car, sounding puzzled but amused.

"Can't you see my angel?" I say, lifting myself carefully off the spot so as not to disturb the shape.

"C'mon in here where it's warm," he says, opening the door and brushing snow off the seat.

I'm grateful. He's turned on the engine, and the car is warm. He gives my shoulders a gruff rub, stifling my chattering teeth. As we leave, I manage a precarious turn and get the car back onto the frozen tracks of a previous driver. His mood is lighter.

"You've changed, you know," he says, his observation coming out of nowhere. "I mean, really changed."

"How so?"

"I don't know exactly," he continues, "just freer. That's it, a free spirit! It's becoming," he says, sounding wistful, as if he wished the same for himself. "How do you do it?"

"There's hardly a choice living here," I say. "Few distractions, no people really. I've been forced to make friends with the outside. Makes you kind of wild."

We're out of the tricky part of the drive, heading across the parking lot, when he asks me to stop the car. "Back up, just a little." He hops out, running into a small wooded area, scarf whipping, hair blowing. When he reappears, he is carrying a pathetic-looking pine tree.

"Don't you think we need a Christmas tree?" he asks, before stuffing the tree inside the trunk. "This one kind of reminds me of us right now."

We both laugh. One spontaneous gesture, and the void begins to fill.

"But we don't have any ornaments," I say. "Oh yes we do," he says, pulling a handful of seashells out of his pocket. "I picked them up while you were still walking."

Together and separately we are making things up as we

go along—a patchwork Christmas-in-the-making. And so the day goes quickly, like most Christmas Eves. There is much to do, even though it's just the two of us. He busies himself jury-rigging the tree while I work on dinner and the stollen. There are various ways to hide from one another, and we've managed to do it in the past—keeping busy, our heads behind books, other people—but today, although working apart, we are collaborating. I feel as playful as that cocky seal, unabashedly floating here and there, drinking a hot toddy and humming holiday tunes. Have I finally used up all my despair? Is all not irretrievably lost?

The Christmas tree is in a flowerpot full of sand. I watch him struggling to string the seashells. His job was always to do the lights, while the boys and I hung the ornaments.

"Want some help?" I ask.

"My fingers aren't as nimble as yours," he responds. He seems happy to hand me the pile of shells and ball of twine.

"So what's tonight's program?" he asks, and immediately I feel resentment. Why is it always my job to create the event and set the scene? "I suppose you want to go to church," he adds. What a stupid statement, I think. Christmas Eve and church are synonymous, aren't they? Why must he even ask? Why doesn't he know what I want?

I could turn his question into a tiff, but I don't, not tonight.

"There's a sweet church nearby," I say, "a simple place. We wouldn't even have to change our clothes."

He takes a swig of his hot toddy. It seems all right with him. We decide on the early service, saving dinner for later.

Even in the best of circumstances, entering a church on Christmas Eve can often distress my psyche, as I am frequently reminded of better and brighter holiday moments. But tonight it looks as if there's going to be a pageant, which might help bring out the child in me. I choke up during the first strains of "O Come All Ye Faithful," its very words suggesting that we all be "joyful and triumphant," but recover quickly upon seeing the Virgin Mary processing past our pew—sneakers on her feet, a wad of gum stuffed in her jowl, and a live baby Jesus slung on her arm as if she'd been a mother forever! Following her are three kings and a queen, assorted bathrobe-clad shepherds, and some fishermen complete with slickers and poles, an obvious gesture for children who know nothing of deserts in the Far East and much of oceans and fish.

I have been in need of something to break in upon my numbness, and the assembling manger scene is doing it. It only gets better as I watch the yawning acolytes who keep forgetting their cues and the little boy who, when the lights are dimmed and the candles lit for "Silent Night," exclaims loudly, "It's Christmas!" Being so disarmed, my guard down, the boy's delight in turn unleashes the child in me.

We exit before the benediction, not wanting the moment to evaporate into bright lights and people chattering. I tuck the bulletin into my pocket in order to read and reread the evening's prayer:

"Forgive our foolish and wandering ways. Open us
anew, stir us and move us to grow . . ."

My cheeks are glowing from the warmth of it all, and what settles over the cottage upon our return are uncomplicated feelings of tenderness. We exchange gifts: He offers his mother's diamond earrings made to fit my pierced ears, a wall hanging displaying business cards of ten accomplished women with a blank space left for my card, and a ceramic seal with a Christmas wreath around its neck. I give him a simple watercolor of our home back in New York, complete with the boys playing basketball in the driveway and our cat on the front porch.

Even our conversation is peppered with a redemptive spirit. When he utters a throwaway comment about our bad marriage (meant to be a joke), I scoop it up before it hits the trash basket, saying, "It's the relationship that soured; the marriage has been a success. Look what we've accomplished as a team: the people we touched, raising boys who had the courage to commit in an age of no commitment, being good children to our parents—need I go on?"

We've been temporarily relieved of tension, as if the tide had changed and the water were rushing in to quench us both, just in time. Yet I would be a fool to jump into his car and return home with him. While this Christmas has been a gift, the new year and its accompanying resolutions remain a challenge. I don't want to return to the way we were, but welcome the unknown of what we could become.

8

GETTING MY
FEET WET

New Year's Eve

*Each first of January that we arrive at is an imaginary
milestone—at once a resting place for thought and meditation, and a
starting place for fresh exertion in the performance of our
journey. The man who does not at least propose to himself to be
better this year than he was last must be either very good
or very bad indeed.*

—Charles Lamb

It *is* the first night of the new year and the last night of the old, and I'm standing in the center of town wearing number 76, surrounded by a hundred or so lean and mean runners, reluctantly waiting for a two-mile road race to begin. Whatever possessed a nonathletic, overweight, middle-aged hypochondriac to do such a thing? It must have been the ad I kept seeing for this event, the one that dared me to greet and meet myself in a new way. I've known for some time that I needed to get out of my head and into my body, and this race seemed to offer me a perfect starting point.

Not only is it a road race, but to add to the element of fun it is a costumed event. I'm dressed in a red warm-up suit with a Christmas tablecloth dangling from my shoulders to look like Little Red Riding Hood. I even brought along a basket to hold and a bonnet to wear. To say I look ridiculous is an understatement. The more experienced runners have donned pitiful accessories such as baseball caps, signs on their shirts, and eyeglasses with plastic noses; nothing that will impair their running prowess.

I've never been in a race before and am more than self-conscious. I move my leaden body away from the crowd so as to consider how I might flee, making comparisons with the other runners, seeing my imperfections, envying their trim physiques, noticing their well-worn sneakers. The few times I remember feeling comfortable in my skin were when I was three or four, all round and dimpled, or during pregnancy when the lack of dips and curves was acceptable. But no sooner were the babies born than my abdomen went from taut to soft, like bread dough, and I reverted to hating my body. No matter that the stretch marks I now boast have my children's names imprinted on them or that I had just finished carrying and creating new life! All that was reflected in the mirror were sagging breasts, minimal waist, a pear-shaped person who was no longer sexy or desirable.

Well, today I am here to face my gross negligence and mend the breach between body and mind. I retire to a nearby parking meter in order to lean on it while I do some stretches. It has always been an annual resolution to work on my body, but resolve usually fades by the end of January. This year seems different, though, and I no longer intend to hide my feelings and aspirations in fat. I want to stand whole in my skin and fly. I'm in a race against time. I need my body to catch up with all of me, to test my will and endurance.

Just then, as I am pulling my foot up to my buttock, my right knee gives out. I shudder in spasm, freezing for a moment to allow the joint to relax before letting go of my foot.

God, I've missed a lot. I should have loved my body better before this race. But physical prowess was not something I was taught to seek. Both my mother and grandmother put limitations on their bodies (or was it done for them?). Hell, when they gave birth, they were thoroughly drugged, such meager faith did doctors place in the workings of their bodies. Imagine, they were denied the one really glorious moment when a woman's body can truly shine. It's no wonder my forebears gave me so little support for my own physical being.

I stopped using my body after the hopscotch period of life, avoided gym class for fear of messing up my hair, wouldn't be caught dead sweating, as it was considered un-feminine. My body became a stranger I chose not to know. Although attached to it like a Siamese twin, I paid it no at-tention, disgusted as I was with its smells, covering up its eruptions, denying its effluvia. My body became no more than a piece of granite to be chipped away at until it became an acceptable shape. I tucked all my insecurities and unre-solved emotions into muscles and joints, which now ache from atrophy.

The various doctors I saw along the way contributed to my bodily aversions. One internist, after hearing a functional heart murmur, sent me off for thousands of dollars' worth of tests that resulted in nothing except a severe case of anxi-ety. Then there was the obstetrician who told me to cross my legs when I was in the final stages of labor while he delivered a woman's twins in the next bed. And my children's pediatri-cian, who enjoyed feeling up his patients' mothers every time they came to the office. These men hardly evoked a sense of trust in themselves or in my body. After a time I simply began to deny I had a body at all and stopped going to doc-tors, which only served to fuel a much more insidious kind of denial that resulted in less maintenance and care.

But then my body began sending me messages, pounding clues about its needs into my bones and flesh. The first signs attacked my lower back, forcing me to take to bed for days until the spasms subsided. There were frequent headaches that hit each time I became obsessive or unrealistic about deadlines. And finally shingles that attached themselves to my ribs and hips and appeared each time I suffered a loss or rejection. Years of denial, coupled with increasing pain, eventually made me take notice, as if a child were tugging at my sleeve pleading for attention. My body was telling me to stop living one way and start considering another. I suppose that's the real reason I'm standing here shivering in the cold, choosing to do something ridiculous or at least downright embarrassing. I need to give my body a mind of its own, to lift the restrictions I have placed on it, to try for once to treat it as if it were all right and normal, whatever that might be.

I move back into the crowd of runners and take a position on the side, near the back of the pack. The day is mine, seize it or miss it altogether. Then this stunning bit of math: I'm fifty. I'll be lucky if I reach eighty. I have 360 months left!

Just then the starting gun explodes and I tentatively push off, muscles trembling, employing a queer bounding gait. But with ample cheers from the crowd feeding the thrill of the moment, I soon become like a horse in a stampede, wanting to run fast, following the leader. The first half mile is a gradual decline, thank God, hardly taxing. I make a pitiful attempt to leap ahead, keeping my stomach tucked in, spine straight, as long as the crowd is watching. But in a matter of minutes my body retaliates from the abuse and neglect; my hamstrings fail to extend, and my calf muscles cramp. As I round the corner of Main and School Streets and spot the hill I must climb, I tell myself I can't.

Still, I'm distracted from the pain by the jungle of

bodies around me. I focus on fannies as they shift and jiggle with each step, observe the ripened, swaying breasts on the larger women and the pancake-flat stomachs on the slight ones, wondering how they can contain their insides in such svelte shells. In contrast, I run in a body I deserve, and just now I feel gravity tugging at me, inches of fat slivering downward from stomach to pelvis to thighs until it settles into my feet, making them feel like five-pound bags of sugar.

I'm following the leader, many leaders, and by now most of them have passed me by as I trip over my feet and slow to a crawl. It's a relief to be running alone, no more comparison, no more competition.

I hate competition. Once I was waiting to appear on a television show to promote a book I was sure would be unpopular, when I gazed at the monitor and heard another author profess that her book had already sold half a million copies. I turned to a stranger nearby and asked, "How can I possibly follow her?" She took me by the shoulders, looked me square in the eye, and said, "Don't compare!"

Okay. Okay. So today I won't compare either; I'll find my own style. But then another hill! I thought this damn town was flat! Only when you meet the road, foot to pavement, do you really become acquainted with the terrain. I'm overwhelmed with the need to quit as the blood carries messages across my pulse points, and I think I may die. The loneliness of the long-distance runner is becoming clear to me. What a dumb idea this was!

But like a woman about to give birth, who doesn't want to do it just yet, I am faced with the reality that I must finish what I started. I gulp some cold air, thinking it will freeze inside me, and run on. A lady cop in a patrol car cheers me on. "Way to go!" she shouts, honking her horn, flashing her lights. She looks about my age, a bit overweight. Maybe she's wishing she had tried to run as well. As I feel her encouragement, I decide to continue for both of us. I nod and wave, amazed that I have enough energy to do so, and think I can't *become* unless I *do*. Then the words from my favorite children's book, *The Little Engine That Could*, pop into my head and give me a subtle rush: *"I think I can, I think I can."*

I've worn too many clothes, a sweatsuit no less. Even so, I'm sure my perspiration will soon become icicles dangling from my armpits and upper lip. How could I know that running in twenty-degree weather would make me hot? Relax your shoulders, Joan, widen your stance a bit, forget your fanny and breathe. What a mean trick I'm playing on this body! A tight body can't suddenly be loose. I've kept it chained and constrained for so long, that suddenly released from its bondage, it is spastic. You can't just one day order a body to do what you need at the moment; a relationship must develop. I must make friends with this stranger that is speaking to me with whines, creaks, and groans, coming to life after thirty-five years of slumber, a woman turned inside out, just now in touch with what once was invisible.

Real fatigue is setting in, but there is mercy. I spot the finish line, pull my shoulders back, throw my chin to the sky, and relax my hips. As I hammer toward the finish, I experience a gush of energy, instead of the strain and tension of the start.

Then it's over. I stagger to a nearby bench, briefly register the genuine applause from the remaining spectators, and collapse. Lost in exhaustion, coughing the chill from my chest, I try to breathe rhythmically again. If I entered this race to escape numbness, I've certainly succeeded.

It's a strange victory I've won. What began as a dare has now become a breakthrough. My father always said that if it wasn't tough, then it wasn't right. Today I had a choice: to grab the day or to be victimized by it. The gift was being given a chance to go beyond my perceived limits. I trusted the unknown, relied on a body I had been taught to fear, and it more than surprised me. I shall give up the idea of having a fashionable body, or an Olympian body. I just want a body that works, that is durable and resilient, that can climb a mountain, carry grandbabies on its back, be vital and energized even after a long day.

A noise parade is assembling in the adjacent park, a motley group of revelers carrying pots and pans, cymbals and sticks. They will create a crazy clatter, their purpose being to drive away that which is old, to let go of the old demons and make room for the new. It occurs to me that I have just been initiated into the second half of my life, crossing the threshold of my past, heading toward unknown frontiers that will inevitably lead me to myself.

I used to feel sad on New Year's Eve, clinging to the old year, never wanting it to be over. I avoided good-byes for the same reason, clinging to what was, simply because it was *known*, whereas the future was *unknown* and therefore to be worried over. How much fear has controlled my life. No longer!

My cheeks sting, and my fingers prickle. I duck into a nearby watering hole and order a hot cider, comfortable this day sitting among strangers. I pat my firm thighs and promise to banish further negative thinking. Smug about my New Year's resolutions, I raise my glass to being big, beautiful, feminine, and forever changing, promising to work with my bones and flesh. After all, bones make new bones if they are exercised, skin sheds itself to make room for fresh flesh, muscles untangle and restore their strength. I truly have rejoined the human race.

9

FOGGED IN

February

I wake to sleep, and take my waking slow.
I feel my fate in what I cannot fear.
I learn by going where I have to go.

—*Theodore Roethke, "The Waking"*

I am sitting at my grandmother's wobbly old kitchen table, nursing a third cup of coffee after the high point of my day—a brisk four-mile walk. I'm generally contented during my walk, with its simple goals of getting my pulse up and trying to beat yesterday's time. Activities with beginnings, middles, and ends spur me on and offer an adrenaline rush, but when they are over, my mood plummets. Having no clear objective dulls my spirit, and then lethargy sets in, stopping me altogether.

This is a lonelier journey than I expected. In the past few days I've spent inordinate amounts of time watching sand slip through an hourglass—it takes fifteen minutes for the sand to empty out of one end, and then I turn it over and watch as the process begins again. I'm reduced to simply watching time pass me by.

My excuse for today's paralysis is a snowstorm which hit two days ago, knocking out both the power and phone lines. I used to like snow days when the kids were little—when they'd snuggle in bed for an extra hour until I lured them into the kitchen with the smell of bacon and crepes. But being alone and holed up on a dirt path that the town doesn't plow is hardly fun, especially since my firewood is dwindling and I have taken to stealing from the neighbors. I tried to hack away at an old fallen tree in the backwoods, but there weren't enough hours of daylight to chop the amount of wood I would need to keep the stove burning for even one night.

My anxiety increases with each passing day—what do I have to show for my half year of seclusion anyway? I'm putting the finishing touches on two children's books, but after that my professional future is uncertain. My collaborator of twelve years up and left, moved cross-country with little or no consideration for the reputation we had developed or the amount of money we generated together. If I hope to salvage my career (which I'm not at all sure I do), I'm left to find myself a new photographer. It feels like a divorce, yet another of last year's many losses, which have left me with a raw, lingering ache.

Certainly the most devastating blow was my father's death, after which I had no time to cry. My mother and her widowhood took precedence over my grief. What's more, I lost my relationship with my only sibling along the way—a brother whose second wife had no use for any part of his family history that did not include her. I hated my brother for not coming to our father's funeral, which sparked a series of arguments that culminated in his throwing me out of his house and his life forever. Stale marriage aside, so much unfinished grieving must surely contribute to my stagnation now. Perhaps I shouldn't chastise myself so much for wandering from room to room, nibbling on stale Christmas cookies, starting projects but not finishing them. I want to trust the hours, but waste them instead. I've never been so close to myself, but somehow we can't seem to make friends.

I did make an attempt to find me last week when I came across a box of childhood snapshots, the box top startlingly labeled THE PAST. I spent an entire day mesmerized by my metamorphosis—spreading the little black-and-white photographs the length of the living-room floor, arranging them in chronological order, looking sometimes with a magnifying glass for telling expressions. Until I was six or seven I appear the epitome of innocence, security, and wonder: frolicking in the snow, at the beach, in the backyard; climbing trees; hanging from jungle gyms; riding my tricycle—always with my brother by my side.

But then we moved—away from our childhood home of Buffalo, New York, to the hills of Pennsylvania, then seventeen more times, each move eliminating more of our history, further uprooting our formative selves until a permanent outsiderness set in. Suddenly, as I gazed at my life on the living-room floor, I saw a little girl with a distant look in her eyes, one who was once tiny and perky, now chubby and sad, a forced smile replacing the earlier easy one, a tense, fearful, yet brave look on her face—as if it was taking every impulse she had to keep herself together. Eventually, in the teenage pictures, I saw a pretty yet rigid person I did not remember, but a persona I recall acting out. Not only did moving catapult me into strange lands, it also wrenched me away from a neighbor lady—a childless woman who loved me unconditionally—who had become a veritable second mother.

Being displaced time and again must contribute to a deeper inner displacement, so that after a while familiar images and values all but slip away. I saw in those pictures that I fitted in and survived by being what those around wanted me to be, leaving the real me by the wayside with permanent scars on her self-confidence. I need to grab her by the hand and make up for lost time, or at least honor her determination and stubbornness—attributes that she displays in the pictures.

"Surely I am lost enough to find myself," I say, repeating the words from a Robert Frost poem. Enough dancing around the edges of newness, Joan! No more treading softly on the back roads of consciousness—circumventing the issues, hoping they will go away. I shake my dismal thoughts and sit Indian style on the floor, eyes closed, rocking back and forth, closing my eyes, shutting off my mind, which too often tempts me into the games of deception I play with myself.

I reopen my eyes and see hanging in front of me a cross that I bought in New Mexico. It's made of scraggy mesquite, crooked and ragged, not straight and narrow. I like its undefined edges. I stare at its hammered-tin center, thinking that at this moment I am at a crossroads that offers three paths (the one behind me represents the past to which I cannot return). The shorter arm to the left leads to my husband, clearly not a place I choose to go. Two other possibilities remain, their destinations unknown. A quiet presence overtakes me, and my pulse slows. My hands relax, and my palms open spontaneously as I am reduced to blessed clarity. I feel a subtle yearning for adventure, similar to the way I felt last fall. Haven't I been counting on seeing new paths? Don't they abound everywhere, out here?

I'm reminded of the words of a Jungian analyst who spoke to a group of women about just such crossroads.

"Many of us would just as soon have our choices made for us," she said, "but the heroine, when at a juncture, makes her own choice—the nonheroine lets others make it for her."

Somewhere in all this muted splendor there must be something that wants me to find it. Why do I dally? I gaze out the window at a thick fog—the Gulf Stream must be blowing its warm wind across yesterday's frozen land, replacing the stark whiteness with a murky gray. The mounds of frozen snow have turned to slush. Perhaps escape is possible.

A foghorn beckons—it's been moaning all morning. Perhaps I'm meant to answer the call, give some value back to my day, leave the safety of the center. I don my yellow slicker, hop into the car, and plow through piles of slush, skidding my way out onto the main road, following the sound as if it were a mother calling her children home, the depth of her howl guiding even the most hopelessly lost back to safety. I'm being pulled toward town and the beach. Once there, I walk gingerly, barely able to see my hand in front of my face. When I round the bend in the road where there is usually a clear view of the sea, I can hear the surf and follow the sound of the water's motion, picturing her foamy waves, soon plunging my boots into the thick, slightly frozen sand.

Trust takes over in the fog, making me think about each step, demanding that senses be finely tuned. I move with determination, though, as I know this place and carry an invisible map in my head. Just now there is no past, no future, only the present. I push on toward the shoreline, planning to follow its lead. I am at the periphery of nowhere, enveloped in heavy mist, moving to the rhythm of undulating water, heading toward a jetty that protrudes far out to sea—a sacred place, really. It is a strong arm of protection for the harbor, an isolated peninsula, perfect for contemplation, a place where no one is likely to find you and try to change your course. I accomplish the mile-long walk in no time and climb upon the rocks, tiptoeing from one to the other, treading carefully as the splashing high tide creates a slippery surface. Utterly alone and feeling devilishly free, I begin to relish my solitary adventure, when suddenly I am startled by the chiseled profile of an aged woman standing tall, a black cape flowing behind her.

She turns her sparkling blue eyes on me as I approach. "Well, hello there. Are we the only ones in this town in a fog?" she quips, laughing at her own joke.

"I guess so," I answer. "How do you do? I'm Joan Anderson."

"I'm Joan, too," she answers, feeling no need to add a surname. "I'm new here. Isn't this a wonderful place?"

I only nod, entranced by her gracefulness—delicate face, high cheekbones, a patrician nose. I'm mystified to find such an elderly person perched on the edge of the world. My sense tells me that she is eighty-five or ninety—her right hand clasps a gnarly wooden cane, partially hidden by her long indigo jersey dress.

"Shall we walk?" she asks, already moving, beckoning me to follow. A few gulls squawk at our invasion, but we march on, drawn by the sound of the channel marker that sits at the very tip of the jetty. The farther we go, the less we can see of the harbor or beach. A small dory has broken away from its mooring and is being smacked against the jetty with each roll of a wave. "I feel a bit like that little boat," I blurt, not meaning to speak my intimate thoughts out loud.

"How's that?" she asks.

"I feel loosened, even free, but with no oar to steady the boat just now."

"I'd say I'm at sea as well," she admits, "but I just keep going. Don't look back—look out. I've left lots of stuff back on shore, hoping I'll find more out here."

"The fishermen think like that," I add. "They go out day after day, trusting the voyage, casting their nets on a whim, and always seem to come up with something."

"It's about action and touch," she says, as if she knows. "That's where the wisdom is—in the senses—stepping out on a gray day, daring to be different. There's no one as foolish as us right now. Thank goodness! We can be in a fog all by ourselves! I love the grayness of it. The mist sort of wraps itself around our thoughts, so they can take hold."

"Never thought about it that way," I say, navigating more cautiously, as waves now splash all about us. The formlessness of the fog encompasses us. We are without shape and design, simply fluid and expansive. To be walking with a fragile dowager, in a precarious spot, challenges me to dare to go farther.

"Sometimes I think women are like the fog," I comment.

"How do you mean, dear?"

"We have a knowledge of what is underneath, but our real selves are obscured by what others think of us."

"Well, I suppose that's so. The mysterious female—we'd best keep it that way."

I laugh at her gentle feminism. "I've been out here a hundred times and never come across the likes of you," I say, reaching out to help her across a gap in the rocks.

"It's all right, Mommy," she says, rejecting my help. "This old body hasn't failed me yet," she adds puckishly, all but dancing over the rough spots.

"How do you keep so well oiled?" I ask.

"Oh, my dear, that's easy. Movement, lots of movement. I walk a couple of miles each day. My body's my main strength, so I'm diligent about taking care of it."

We arrive at the end and lean against the base of the channel marker. Her thoughts are delicious. I want to know more—could listen to her all day. *When the pupil is ready, the teacher appears*, so the saying goes. And to think I hesitated before venturing out today.

She seems to share my feelings and surprises me by saying, "I like you! What do you do, anyway?"

I fill in the blanks of my life—married, two boys, a writer of children's books—and tell her that I've come here to find myself.

"Well, you sure can find a self out here, I should think. I've never been able to substitute words for experience—just got to get out and do it, like we're doing now." Her words are as soothing as the lighthouse beam that now cuts through the fog—steady, strong, alive—a focal point amid the gray.

Eventually we begin to make our way back from where we came, walking single file. "I'd be delighted if we could meet again," she says. "Perhaps have some port, late one afternoon."

"I'd like that," I say, as we approach the parking lot where a taxi is waiting to take her home, wherever that is.

"I hate not having a car," she says, clearly not happy having to be driven around. "I'm looking into getting a golf cart this spring—that and a three-wheel bicycle."

I shake my head in disbelief. Never have I seen such determination in someone so old. "Your last name—tell me how I can find you," I say, as she gracefully ducks into the backseat. "Erikson," she answers. "Joan Erikson. I live up Bank Street on Parallel. Call me, will you, dear?" And with that the door slams and she is gone.

I am smitten. For such a long time I've been wishing to stumble upon someone who might point the way, or at least hint at it. It occurs to me that being in the fog does not have to mean being altogether lost.

10

SEAL WOMAN

March

In the beginning there was thought and her name was woman.

She is the OLD woman who tends the fires of life.

She is the OLD woman spider who weaves us together.

She is the eldest God and the one who remembers and

RE-MEMBERS.

—*Anonymous*

She $appeared$ in my life like a full-moon tide whose frothy waves smack upon the shore, trickling upward, refreshing the toes of the beachcomber. After our first encounter, our next—complete with an orange-and-purple sunset and several glasses of port—sealed the friendship, lifting the fog that had encapsulated me.

I was reticent, even shy at our first few meetings, having noticed her late husband's picture on the cover of *Time* hanging over her desk—the famed psychoanalyst Erik Erikson, who coined the term "identity crisis." Celebrity unsettles me, making me wonder if I can measure up. I had to stifle the desire to impress and, instead, strive to give in to just being me, with all my inadequacies. Fortunately, Joan reassured me that perfection had also eluded her. In any case, I had no choice as to whether or not I would be her friend; she had attached herself to me, as I had to her, like an oyster to a rock. We would be "stuck" as long as no storm came along and tore us away—me and an old woman with the heart of a young girl, opening her heart because she thought us kindred spirits.

Real connection seems to happen that way—two like-minded souls meet and sniff around one another like puppy dogs, then *whoosh*, a moment of fission occurs, pleasantries are dropped, closely twined feelings surface, and a relationship is born. It's been six weeks since that afternoon on the jetty; we're past the beginner phase of friendship, eager to jump into the deeper places where intimacies and vulnerabilities lie waiting to be shared.

"If we can't share our real feelings, we might as well be men," she joked one day last week, dropping one of her verbal nuggets. "Everybody is soooo serious, when actually we're all a joke."

Being "stuck" with my new friend is like having Tinker Bell or Cinderella's fairy godmother stop by and insist on being of service. I have always had an affinity for magical creatures, for their power to transform mundane individuals into liberated spirits. It is as if I've been kissed by a muse—not of the Prince Charming variety, but rather, a ninety-two-year-old lady who spins out her wisdom, expecting me to catch the vibrations.

"Leave room for yourself," she insists as we spend several afternoons working together on handheld looms. She has taught me how to weave, and now we are creating small tapestries that represent the stages of our lives. I was characteristically rushing the process, combining the colors too quickly without really absorbing what each one meant: qualities such as autonomy, initiative, industry, intimacy. "You must look more carefully at what it means when one color meets another," she says, "to see how many strengths you have to work with and lean on."

Through her I am beginning to see that every thread is significant. To think of pulling out a color here or adding one there would be to alter the fabric of who I am. She is teaching me that the delight is in the continuum—to take all that I know and am and weave that wisdom into the fabric of everyday life, remembering always to leave room for myself. "Please, dear," she's had to say to me more than once, "keep the weaving tight so that you have space for what you're becoming. You've covered two thirds of the loom, and you still have half your life left."

Every woman should have a mentor—not her mother, but someone who doesn't have a stake in how she turns out, who encourages her to risk, who picks her up when she falls flat on her face. Joan prods, pokes, and coaxes me each time we're together, like a mother trying to waken her sleepy child to get her off to school in time. Her phone calls come early, during the twilight state between dreaming and waking.

"Hi, dear," she says, her voice as soothing as warm maple syrup. "Want to get into some trouble today?"

"What did you have in mind?" I ask, smiling at her devilishness.

"Oh, I don't know—just getting out and gathering up some experiences!"

Today's outing will be a hike through a nearby moor. Around noon I drive to her tiny house, which is nestled beside a marsh, and bow to a statue of St. Francis, whose duty is the safekeeping of the multiple species of birds that come to eat at one of her various bird feeders. In lieu of a doorbell she has a metal triangle hanging from a hook beside the front door, with written instructions dangling from its wand: RING VIGOROUSLY. Several clangs later she appears, comfortably dressed in her at-home uniform—tights, sensible black sneakers, and a jacket that she made out of her husband's old ties.

"Hello," she exclaims, opening her arms, pulling me into

a hug. I embrace her gently, fearful of brittle bones. "Oh, no, you don't," she whispers, sensing I'm holding back, and she hugs me more firmly. "Come in. I've something to read to you." She takes my hand, leads me down a hallway, past the treadmill and a makeshift altar for her dancing Buddha, then into the sparsely furnished living area, where a giant piece of driftwood is the only adornment.

I settle onto a wicker stool near her feet, as she straddles a swivel seat near her desk, which is awash in a glorious confusion of cubicles stuffed with notes, lovely stationery, fountain pens, and a sign pasted to her lamp that says, SMILE ANYWAY. "Now, let's see, where's the damned thing?" she says, fumbling through papers until she locates the one. "I wrote a poem for you last night. Tell me what you think."

RECOMMENDATION

Impatient lady, eager now to know
To traffic with that bird of night
Before even early frost has touched your hair.
An open mind has depths that grow
Only as shadows to the light,
Let be what is Becoming—slowly
Slowly grow and know, Patience.

I squirm a bit, knowing she has tapped into my haste— my need to find answers *now*. Although she hasn't pried into my life—what I'm doing here without a husband—I'm sure she senses my struggle. "Patience isn't your virtue, is it, dear?" she says, filling the quiet moment between us. "You mustn't fret. There is no arriving, ever. It is all a continual be-coming."

Tears fill my eyes as I recognize that she is seeing the real me.

"So much of you is waking up," she adds. "I see you bubbling all over the place—you're yeasty, and I think it's grand!"

I suppose she's right, although I still can't shake the stagnation that overwhelms me every time I think about the future.

"You must have been so careful with what you did and said in your former life, so as to stifle the very essence of you. No wonder you're here, and in a hurry."

Tears trickle down my flushed cheeks, as I am relieved to be found out. I've always wanted to know someone who would bother to see beyond the surface of me, without my giving many clues.

As if she knows what I'm thinking, she says, "It's the way they want us, you know—predictable and appropriate. Trouble is, we end up being apropos of nothing!"

We both laugh, dispelling any gloom. This is the first time since coming here that I feel affirmation for my decision. "It was so hard to leave home," I tell her, "but instinct told me to travel to where nature might take its course."

"Me, too," she offers. "I came here, leaving friends and Cambridge behind, to deal with my husband's infirmity without interference. You are never free to do as you please when you stay with the familiar."

I find our situations curious. She ran away *with* her husband, I *from* mine. I wish my inclination had included him, but it didn't. Before I can sink into disdain, she rescues my mood.

"Being here is a sound choice, dear—not hiding under the covers like so many wives do, sniveling, afraid of losing their security. So many women believe that love is a feeling of being dependent. Sometimes having a husband can be a sort of alibi for a woman. Look, you've slammed one door, but oh, how you've opened another! People develop in aloneness and are only led to the truth after being disillusioned."

My panic subsides as she continues.

"I've been running away, all my life," she says. "When I was little, I ran to the woods—only place I could be my-self—then off to Europe—unheard of for a woman of twenty-one—changed my name and became whatever and whoever I wanted. You've got to be your own person. In any case, it's pretty deadly not to be! Honey, it takes action to create change. Everything we talk about isn't worth a dime if we don't actualize it."

"So what are we waiting for?" I say. "You keep talking about overdosing on the senses. Shall we get going?"

"It's high time," she agrees, grabbing her coat, hat, and gloves in order to face the cold, gray afternoon. We are in the car and at Stage Harbor in no time. I park near the light-house, and before I can lock the doors she hops out, heading straight for the desolate moor at a catch-me-if-you-can pace. It's a desolate place, but we think it beautiful, overflowing as it is with hearty lichen, bayberry shrubs, grasses—a place abundant with signs of beginnings. Here the visitor is tempted not just to stretch, but to grow new as well.

We pretend we're on a treasure hunt for our souls,

looking for nothing in particular but hoping to find that piece of shell or rock or driftwood that speaks to us. The winter's storms have deposited inordinate amounts of seaweed everywhere, which makes navigating feel as though we are walking on a giant sponge. I see her in the distance, bending down to pick up a handful of weed. She turns to see if I'm looking, then drapes a bunch of it over her head. "I always dreamed of being a mermaid," she shouts, wryly amused at her own folly and her new mass of tangled hair. "What do you suppose people would say if they could see what passes between us?"

It occurs to me that she is a native of these elements—familiar with them in some intimate way. Just now her manner reminds me of the seals. They hear what others cannot, have knowledge of what is underneath, are energized by the wild. Is that who Joan is, after all: a seal woman who traverses the worlds of humans and animals alike? In any case, her antics never fail to strip away adulthood and reduce me to childishness. Suddenly there is playfulness and light. Who cares where water stops or wind begins?

I spot a red fox staring into a puddle not ten feet from where we stand and grab Joanie's arm to alert her. Within seconds the creature notices us, and we stand eyeball to eyeball for a solid minute, after which the fox turns back to the puddle, more interested in her own reflection than in the likes of us. "Good for you," Joan says, applauding the fox. "We could all stand a little more reflection."

We move toward a hollow where thousands of bleached shells and other souvenirs of sea life are scattered about.

Poking with her cane, she loosens one object, then another—the more broken and ravaged, the better. I sit contented on a nearby log and peruse this solitary place. "Would be a great place for a vision quest," I think out loud.

"What's that?" she asks, continuing to scavenge while I talk.

"I had it explained to me by a Navajo elder a few years ago. He takes to the wilderness once a year and spends twenty-four hours in one solitary spot, while nature offers itself to him. He told me that even the most cluttered mind is emptied of extraneous thought after the first hour, and that a true language comes out of silence."

"This would be a fine place," she agrees, sounding eager to participate in such a thing, right now.

I move away, withdrawing into my own space, having found some beach glass and now want to look for more. As I finger the pieces in my pocket, I realize that once they were part of a whole. Now they are cracked and broken, but time has softened their edges, each becoming new on their own—a nice metaphor for a woman who has evolved through various passages, integrating the soft and the hard sides of her personality, now beginning to relax into understanding what her life is all about.

Today a quahog shell, complete with a hinge holding a fragment of its other half, teases me to pick it up. It has a regality about it, a triumphal purple band embedded in its edges. I imagine the juicy center it once had and think such a shell is like a woman who spends years holding her family members together, then becomes unhinged when they're gone, like the clam, no longer needing to be so attached to the other half; not unlike a husband and wife in a long-standing marriage, both pursuing that which is unlived about their lives.

My nose directs me next to a cluster of toenail shells wilting on the drying sand, clinging to one another. I am struck by the stench that comes from such clinging, holding on when it might have been better to let go. How many people have I clung to or let cling to me long after it ceased to be a healthy thing to do? Part of the freedom I feel today comes from letting go.

After a while Joan comes to me, taking hold of my hand without asking, and we stand facing the sea with all the vastness it offers. We are helping each other be real people; her need for companionship, so she can have freedom and adventure, forces me to go after the same. Our treasure hunts rarely reveal a single insight of great importance. Rather, we come away with new attitudes. As for me, my energy is redirected, my humor returns, body and mind are stretched.

Eventually we head home, two wash-ashores who have taken a seaside cure, more refreshed than when we arrived.

11

EBB AND FLOW

April

If you can talk with crowds and keep your virtue,
Or walk with Kings—nor lose the common touch;
If neither foes nor loving friends can hurt you;
If all men count with you, but none too much;
If you can fill the unforgiving minute
With sixty seconds' worth of distance run—
Yours is the Earth and everything that's in it,
And—which is more—you'll be a Man, my son!

—Rudyard Kipling, "If"

I *am* standing in the kitchen on an early-spring morning, hands in soapy water, tackling a sinkful of dirty dishes from last night's feast, one of many I've prepared this month for the smorgasbord of people that has appeared on my doorstep, melting my carefully drawn boundaries as quickly as the ice has dissolved on the pond.

These random intrusions began innocently enough, with day visits from an old college roommate and a distant cousin in search of a cottage to rent for the summer. Soon thereafter the entertaining got more serious: relatives of Joan Erikson for a weekend, a visit from my good friend Hazel, and eight days of dinner parties for an independent film crew. I am being forced to stop being in solitude!

As I stack the plates, hand-dry the glasses, and sort the flatware, I keep glancing at the little weaving Joan and I did, which hangs on the wall over the sink, and wonder if, as she so often urges, I've left room for myself during these visits or given in to the demands of the crowd?

Although I was apprehensive about company of any kind, Joan's description of her cousin and his wife, coming east to attend a conference, was thoroughly tempting; he is a psychoanalyst and she an Episcopal priest. How could I not take them in? I felt it was time to open my door anyway, to let in fresh thoughts. There was a special appeal to playing hostess to a shrink as I began to imagine all the questions I could ask him about my psyche.

His wife unnerved me at first, until I realized that she was merely studying my character, making sure that Joan had fallen into good hands. He, on the other hand, stripped away my armor in no time, an affable sort of guy eager for involvement, who asked *me* questions, rather than the other way around.

They arrived after dark, and as we shared wine, cheese, and our life stories well into the night, I remembered how good conversation has forever been an aphrodisiac. Our talk turned to Jungian philosophy, as we discussed balancing the feminine and masculine in our personalities, working with one's shadows, and other such erudite topics.

"At our ages and stages we should be going for the gold of our shadows," he said. "Look at the dirt in your life and work with it, instead of avoiding it."

"Wait a minute," I inserted, not holding back as I often do to hide my ignorance. "First things first—what the hell is my shadow?"

"Your dark side, the evil stuff about you," he answered. "Here's an example: I might be attracted to a twenty-one-year-old client, not an unusual occurrence for a man my age, and yet if I acted on my lustful fantasies there might be all hell to pay. But simply denying these thoughts is sheer repression. I might have had to turn off such thoughts when I was newly married and we were raising our children, but now I have more freedom and will gain nothing from denying my fantasies. Rather, it behooves me to bring them to the surface, look at what I might be missing, and then move ahead to incorporate, say, more passion in my life, within the bounds of my marriage."

I was sitting cross legged on the floor and changed positions, a bit self-conscious now, wondering what he really thought about my leaving my husband, living alone, trying to find myself. I dared to ask, not for his opinion of me, but how someone in my situation works with her shadow.

"You're actually embracing your shadow right now," he said, "by doing something out of the ordinary pattern, looking at stuff you've probably been afraid to unleash for years."

He was right, of course, but I didn't want to say what I was unearthing, because I didn't feel comfortable just now, spilling such thoughts to a relative stranger, no matter how quickly we've become intimate. Even so, each evening with these two was intense and invigorating.

Still, I remained aware that I was the entertainer—the hostess who had the dinner ready when they returned every evening from their conference and vacation time, the one doing most of the planning and work for them, dues I obviously still think I should pay in order to have such experiences. So it was shocking when I sat down to record our conversations in my journal and search for the answers we surely must have arrived at after all the talk. When I drew a blank and had nothing to write, I began to wonder if any hard truths had passed between us. Was our talk mostly theory, lacking feeling? Both concerned and then agitated, I went to Joan to discuss why so much effort brought so little return.

"You can't find answers from authorities, silly, especially when they are men!" she said, somewhat disappointed that I hadn't gotten that already. "It's only going to come from here," she insisted, pointing to her heart, "not out there. It's about give-and-take, pulling and tugging, working it through, like our weavings."

I chastised myself all the way back to the cottage for having dumb expectations. Suddenly I was cranky and irritable from all the effort I put forth. Solitude eliminates servitude, that's for sure. Although I love the idea of an open-door policy, and am coming to realize that some helpful lessons can be learned from new people and experiences, I must remember to be kinder to myself. I will launder the sheets and towels, close the door to the guest room, and reclaim my unencumbered space.

Just as I was again getting used to walking around in my underwear and not flushing the toilet if I didn't want to, I heard a car disturbingly close to the cottage. I peered out the kitchen window, expecting a fuel truck or the mailman, only to discover the pixie face of my good friend Hazel behind the windshield of her car. Both anxious and excited about this new interruption, I went out to greet her.

"Your voice sounded awfully flat to me the last time we talked," she confessed, explaining her unannounced arrival. "I was in Boston visiting my aunt Bessie and couldn't resist seeing for myself if you were really all right."

I let her caring sink in. Her coming was a brave move. Despite our eight-year friendship, she still does not trust the fact that I love her unconditionally and would never say no to a visit. Still, there she stood: in a loose-fitting Putumaya dress, her arms loaded with food and gifts, looking more like an aging flower child, complete with Birkenstocks and granny glasses, than the well-established pediatrician she is.

Always paying her way, more than generous, Hazel gives too much, compensating, I suppose, for what she thinks she lacks in personal attributes. How could such an accomplished woman be so short on self-esteem? I wondered, then laughed. We are the same. Perhaps that's the reason we're friends, why I wasn't put off by her arrival. Hazel is as hungry for approval and affection as I am; we both have much to give each other.

"I last saw you as you drove away from New York," she said wistfully when we settled into an evening of catching up. "I was so jealous. I still am, come to think of it, now that I see what you were going to."

"But you couldn't run away if you wanted to," I reminded her, "married as you are to your pediatrics practice and that husband of yours, who you can't stop trying to please."

She only nodded, offering no comment. We usually save husband and children talk for last, after we've covered the details of our own lives. "How long can you stay?" I asked, hoping maybe for a couple of days.

"Just the night," she answered, "although once I take residence in that cozy loft guest room of yours, I may never leave. It feels like a tree house."

We got into the pissing-and-moaning phase of the evening while making dinner and getting a little drunk. I'd forgotten how much fun it was to have someone to complain and gossip with, to make those inevitable comparisons between our lives and those of mutual friends. We like our rebellious friends best and have less patience for those who hesitate to risk. We cheer on the ones who stumble regularly, endure false starts, and couldn't be perfect if they tried.

The next morning more of the same chatter continued over the breakfast Hazel had whipped up, blueberry pancakes "full of bran and whole-wheat flour," she insisted, "not at all fattening."

"Next time you've got to stay longer," I told her as she prepared to leave. Tears, partially hidden behind sunglasses, stained her cheeks as we said good-bye. There is so much relief and comfort in sharing truths with a dear friend—being with someone with whom you don't have to justify everything.

Her visit affirmed the life I have chosen to live and the limits I have set. She did not stay beyond her welcome or ask me to play hostess. She offered me time and companionship and, as usual, left behind a pile of books I was supposed to read for discussion the next time we met. I was eager to settle back into seclusion just as the phone rang.

"Hey, Joan," my oldest nephew said, "I'm on the Cape, about to shoot a film, and I need to talk to you. Can I come over?"

"Why not?" I answered, even though I sensed he was after money, shelter, something like that, the operative word being "need." I had half expected to hear from him, as the entire family had been following his fledging film career and I knew his latest script was set by the sea. Still, I was curious as to how I might fit into the picture. He's a master persuader, and I've always been a sucker for his requests since I was actually present for his birth. I braced myself.

A few hours later he arrived with his problem. "The woman I had lined up to cook for the crew got another job," he said. "I need someone in a hurry. Is there any way you'd consider doing it?"

I was momentarily flattered that he had such confidence in me, and I quickly felt that old adrenaline rush that comes from greasepaint. The romance and excitement that surround production are pure heaven for me, a form of speed that always fires me up, taking over my entire personality. Still, he was not asking me to hold the lights, design the set, act in the production. I was, after all, only the cook. I tamed my initial enthusiasm and asked for more details.

"I've got a thousand dollars budgeted for food," he continued, "and minimum wage for the cook. That would be you," he added, pointing to me with an impish grin.

Should I or shouldn't I? Two gorgeous guys, crew members, stood nearby as we talked, their raw ambition contagious. I was about to acquiesce, tempted by the lark of it all and the prospect of some extra cash.

"Is your place large enough to handle the whole crew?" he asked.

"My place!" I hadn't thought where they'd be fed.

"We'll be shooting for the next six days. Lunch is served on location, and then we crash for dinner wherever you prepare it," he added.

My enthusiasm waned the more I contemplated the logistics, as well as the invasion of my carefully calculated privacy. He offered further details, assuming now that I was his for the asking. "Three are vegetarian, six don't eat mayonnaise, one's lactose-intolerant, another is allergic to nuts.

Actually, most of them are into health food," he added, "so have lots of juices, yogurt, and salad stuff."

"Wait a minute," I said, now clearly annoyed by all the restrictions. "You're in a jam and I happen to be available to help out. But I've got my own parameters. You'll get your basic Yankee fare—chowders, fish stews, corn pudding, baked beans. Those with dietary idiosyncrasies will have to fill in with their own stuff. There are limits to my good graces," I countered, surprised, yet pleased for speaking up.

He was pensive for a minute, concerned, not so much for me, but rather with pleasing those in the crew. Still, what choice did he have but to agree with my terms?

"Okay. It's a deal. Thanks for helping out, Joan," he said with a sense of resigned relief. "I've set up an account at the market," he told me. "Sign my name along with yours." And with that, they were off.

My mind raced with menu possibilities as I contemplated the shoestring budget as well as the pampered palates. Tacos with beans and rice instead of beef will be the first meal—a do-it-yourself dinner with very little cooking and a lot of chopping. Other entrees: pizza, vegetarian lasagna, bouillabaisse. I made a list in the car on the way to the market: noodles, cheeses, salad stuff, spaghetti sauce, sour cream, drinks. Drinks! Other than juice, what should I get? I settled on seltzer and cheap wine. One hour later, dragging two grocery carts into the checkout line, I had the ingredients for four dinners and several lunches, and had spent only $492.43.

Mornings were the most hysterical, filled with preliminary dinner preparations and lunch fixings that had to be packed for transport and driven to location, then set up as a buffet in the back of a borrowed Jeep.

But the payoff was being the voyeur, drinking in scene after scene, watching two actors, a director, a female cinematographer, and sound, lighting, and set designers work their magic, some doing it for as little as room, board, and love of the craft. Mostly I was struck by how finely tuned their senses were, all having their own specialties, and how they blended their sensitivities to bring about a unified creation.

How do my sensitivities measure up? Do I truly hear? Am I really aware of the subtleties of light? Do I notice color and form? Perhaps the next time I do something as simple as go to the beach I should take note of what I'm seeing and hearing as if these sights and sounds were to be immortalized on film. In any case, eight days of watching people dig beneath the surface of things, striving to get into the soul of the materials, was nothing short of inspiring.

Beyond that, I saw these troubadours living out their dreams—albeit from hand to mouth, but traveling wherever their next job takes them, working with the unknown and thriving. I don't think I regret leaving the theater business some thirty years ago, but I am glad to be reawakened to the delight of it and reminded that it is never too late to dream.

As I wipe down the counters and take out the garbage, I'm amazed that I survived this social month fairly unscathed. Perhaps that's because I went with the ebb and flow of each visit, allowing for some give-and-take, offering and retreating, weaving myself in and out of each encounter.

I'm not anxious to play bountiful hostess to anyone. But

I will welcome family, good friends, and creative people in small doses and as often as my energy permits.

For now, though, I'm glad to have my time and space back. Tonight I shall open a can of soup and dine happily alone. I'm learning to sponsor myself, no longer the servant but a master of my own time and destiny. It's all about intention—knowing when to open the door and then when to close it again.

12

LOW TIDE

May

One is not born a woman, one becomes one.

—*Simone de Beauvoir*, A WOMAN'S JOURNAL

I've *taken* up clamming, not because I yearn to battle the fickle spring elements of the outer bar, but because I am in dire need of some cash.

The crisis occurred a few weeks back when I went to do a sinkful of dirty dishes and realized that there was no hot water. I headed for the cellar, hoping that the pilot light had been snuffed out, and promptly stepped into an inch of water. The plumber confirmed my worst fear: a leaking water heater. The cost of a new one would be twelve hundred dollars. It has always been difficult for me to ask for help, but I had no choice. I would have to swallow my hard-earned, self-sufficient pride and telephone my husband.

There have been a few friends I've been able to call on because they give without condition, but not my husband, and certainly not now. "If you'd been living with me as I had planned, this wouldn't have happened," he said upon hearing the problem. "Obviously you've overtaxed the water heater. I told you the cottage wasn't properly winterized."

"I know," I say shriveling into silence, feeling weak with surrender, guilty once again for all I'm not doing.

"Look," he continued, "we don't have the money right now. The deal was, I'd keep paying the mortgage on the cottage, and you'd do the rest. This house I rented down here for the *two* of us is draining me financially." Then, with his

Scorpio venom, he added, "Why don't you call on one of your fishermen friends? They seem to be coming through for you."

There was more than a hint of jealousy in his voice, which completely turned me off. My mind flooded with memories of other times he hadn't come to the rescue—the onset of a miscarriage when he left me in pain to attend a board meeting; forgetting to renew the Triple-A card when he knew my old car was constantly breaking down; waiting for me once at the wrong door of the train station while I stood for three hours as my period trickled down my legs.

I wanted to kick myself for calling him, clinging to the infantile fantasy of being rescued, wanting him to feel sorry for me. But as his litany of excuses continued, I simply interrupted. "Never mind. I'll figure something out," and then hung up the phone, determined not to sink.

"I can move through this storm," I repeated under my breath, defiant now. I might crave consensus, but chaos and rejection, filled as they are with fear and hope, offer a high of their own. At the very least, anger incites me to action, which in turn forces me to be creative.

As I ponder my options, I'm inspired by the stories of others in my gene pool—strong women who faced a good deal more than not being able to pay their bills. My grandmother, who left her womanizing husband after an argument and wheeled her two babies in a pram from Brooklyn to Manhattan to take shelter with an aunt; my mother, who lied about her age in order to get employment and move up the ladder on Wall Street; and an aunt who, when her father made her reject a scholarship to a good university, thinking she would only get into trouble, disregarded his dictum and ran off to Europe, where she was free to do as she pleased.

Their collective stories rescue me from any remaining vestiges of victimhood, getting me out of the cottage and heading toward the fish pier with a mind full of job possibilities. I could become a fish baiter, baiting miles of line in order to lessen the fisherman's labor; or pack and ice fish at the cooperative; or get some other odd dock job. The closer I get to the harbor, the more eager I am to *do something*, hopefully something remarkable.

The very act of seeking sets things in motion, my father used to tell me, and he is about to be proven right. No sooner am I in the parking lot than I spot Joshua Cahoon. "I don't believe it's you," I shout out the car window, excited to reconnect with my clamdigger friend. "I haven't seen you since the market closed. How have you been?"

"Not bad, not bad," he mumbles in his slow Yankee drawl. "Now that the weather's turned, I'm getting out to the flats almost every day. And you? Thought you'd be back in the big city by now."

"Nope, not me," I answer smugly. "It has been a good winter, except for right now. I'm a little short of cash."

"You could always try clammin'," he suggests. "Just need to get yourself a license. I'd be happy to loan you a rake and basket."

"What's a license cost?" I ask.

I'm shocked when he says a hundred dollars. "But you'll make that back in a day. Just gotta dig eighty pounds or so. I do that in a couple of hours."

"Sounds like an awful lot to me," I say. "Do you really think I could do it?"

"There's lots of lady clammers," he informs me. "Just takes some will and fortitude. You seem to have plenty of that," he says with an impish wink.

I'm taken aback, not only because he's being unusually communicative, but because he's trying to solve my money crunch.

But with no HELP WANTED signs anywhere in sight, I figure I'd better seize the chance, very much like the surfer who catches the crest of any wave in order to ride to shore. My mother had religiously preached the old adage "Nothing ventured, nothing gained." Without further discussion, I spring for the license and commence digging for my fortune.

Two weeks have gone by. I've been out to the flats now six or seven times, a certified clammer almost, complete with my own rake and a brass growth ring I wear on a leather string around my neck.

The first day was a disaster, with high winds and heavy mist. I tried to learn how to clam while wearing several layers of clothing and a slicker. I was not only discouraged but demoralized, with nothing to show for my labor after the first hour.

Joshua paid me no attention, intent as he was on digging his three hundred pounds' worth. Mercifully, sometime before noon he noticed my predicament and came over to give me some pointers. "First of all, you've got to stomp around a bit—get the clams to spit, which makes holes in the sand. See what I mean?" he said, pointing to all the holes he was generating. "There's clams underneath here." In seconds he was digging briskly with his short-handled rake and popping them out one after another. "You've got to picture just where you think they are and then scoop 'em out. Okay, now you try."

Down I went, body bent over as if to pray, and plunged the rake into a spot with tons of air holes. Then I lifted the wet sand out of the muck—and with it a clam!

"Go on," Josh coaxed, "do it again." Soon I had created several feet of sand mounds, and a string of clams decorated the surface.

"I think you've got it," he cheered, genuinely happy for me. "It won't be so easy in an hour or so. Your arms will hurt, your back will ache, but keep your mind on the money. A basket of clams is worth fifteen or twenty dollars! Set a goal—a bucket would be great for today—and then go after it."

A quick calculation that first day told me this wasn't going to make a dent in my crisis. The plumber would install a new water heater if I put down a third of its cost. At that rate it would take a month of working every day just to get the down payment! I had to dig at least two buckets that first day and then try to increase my haul each time I went out. Desperate, I began digging relentlessly. Beginner's luck was with me. Every strike with my rake rendered a clam or two. I grew exhilarated. "Nothing ventured, nothing gained," I repeated again and again.

An hour of steady work, and I ran out of steam. Having never used my upper body like this, my arms were in spasm. I retreated to the dunes for a sandwich and some coffee. Josh had long since eaten his first lunch—he brings three. "I lost thirty pounds the first year of clamming," he said. "Doesn't look as strenuous as it is."

"So I'm finding out," I quipped, stretching out on the dry dune and raising my arms above my head, careful not to get too comfortable, as I had a bucket and a half still to fill.

"You don't want to stop for very long," Josh warned. "Motion is the only way you'll stay warm."

I rallied and began stomping around like an Indian at a powwow, becoming giddy when I realized that hundreds of clams must be spitting underneath. Back down I went for round two, this time praying to St. Anthony, who finds lost objects, and sure enough I began popping up the little buggers. It was addictive, like eating peanuts; the more I found, the more I wanted to find. By midafternoon I was topping off basket number two.

It took a while to find a slow and steady rhythm, but the more comfortable I became in the role of clammer, the more I relaxed into the flats. Josh sees the flats as his office. To me they feel more like church. There's something spiritual about a span of beach that appears out of nowhere for a limited amount of time and then disappears again, never to resurface in exactly the same way. I'm learning to surrender both to the grueling work and to the isolation. When I need centering, I sing a favorite hymn, "Spirit of God descend upon my heart," which also allows me to eavesdrop on my spirit and pick up on its mumblings.

On bad days what bubbles up is self-loathing. Working in the muck tends to make me focus on my dark side, on all the faults and vices that my husband and others have had to put up with. It depresses me to think that my desire to seek clarity this past year has probably only further complicated my relationship, harmed my husband's ego, and distanced me from my sons. But on sunny days, when my haul is good, my spirit is buoyed. I feel a pride that comes from problem-solving and genuine hard work. Each time I venture to this eerie place, I become a little less of the me I once was—that controlling, stubborn person—and more of the sponta-neous person I want to reclaim.

Joan Erikson applauds my new job. She says work should be play, that anything else is a dead end. "I'm glad you're getting out of your head and into your body, dear. That's when you learn. Theory doesn't mean a damn if you don't actualize it," she repeats. She's right. I hadn't realized how much I enjoy using my hands. Clamming reminds me of when I was a child building sand castles, everything within my grasp and the range of the eye. A task that was at first monotonous has become more creative as I focus on what's before me: uncountable gradations of tone and hue—mauve, black, brown, gray—a world of reflections created on wet sand from the slanted light of a cloudy sky. I'm put into a Zen-like state, often transcending who I was when I arrived at the beginning of each day.

I'm learning that what's important is not so much what I do to make a living as who I become in the process. Simple labor is smoothing my edges, teaching me to crave work not just because it might make me special or wealthy but because the job pleases my spirit, makes me a more pleasant person, and meets my immediate financial needs. These days satisfaction comes from seeing wire clam baskets filled to the brim, three-quarters submerged in a nearby tidal pool some six hours after I arrive at the flats.

Just as the sea has withdrawn to offer us its floor, ever so subtly it returns. At first I notice the dry spot where I stand becoming mush. Then water begins pushing up from underneath, creating rivulets, which grow into tributaries of the mighty ocean. Within minutes water swirls around me.

"Here comes the tide," Josh yells. Sure enough, his little boat, which had been beached, leaning on its side for several hours, has now righted itself and stands ready to take us back to the mainland. I grab my baskets and gear and wade out, ready for the day's end. Timing my day to the tides has helped me stop the frustrating practice of forcing and manipulating my life. I understand now why I was annoyed when a neighbor stopped by the other day with a bunch of forsythia. "Something to brighten your day," she said cheerily, speaking with pride of how she had gathered the branches over a month ago, brought them in to the warmth of her house, and forced the buds to blossom early. I listened, all the while feeling unsettled about what she was telling me. Clamming has taught me that all will be mine in its time and season. Forcing things works against instinct and the elements. It is an art form I was taught to perfect—forced conversation, feelings, orgasms even, prayer—but it is no longer a comfortable way for me to be. Working within the tides and the rules of the universe is fast becoming my preference.

I take one last gulp of the clean air and exhale slowly as Josh starts up the engine. Surrounded by sea life, picking the grit from under my fingernails, licking the salt off my lips, I know, *truly know*, the value of a day, which is made even more apparent when my pockets bulge with cash, soon to be stuffed into a coffee-can bank, partially hidden among food-stuffs in the pantry.

I am cold, wet, achy, yet eager to call the plumber. Today's haul put me over the four-hundred-dollar mark. If he can schedule me for tomorrow, I can finally take a blessed bath! I've made do by leaving a lobster pot full of water on the woodstove in the morning and then dumping it into the tub at night. Tiger balm and cheap wine are the other indulgences that repair my body in time for the next dig. I welcome a real cleansing.

13

TREADING WATER

Memorial Day

It is easy in the world to live after the world's opinion;
it is easy in solitude to live after our own; but the great
man is he who in the midst of the crowd keeps with perfect
sweetness the independence of solitude.

—*Ralph Waldo Emerson, "Self-reliance"*

M*emorial Day* is upon me, with its annual family reunion. Once the boys were married, we picked one weekend a year to gather as a family. This early-summer holiday fits the bill because it lacks ritual and presents no divided loyalties with the in-laws. I considered canceling it this year, given my tenuous situation, but I see the boys so seldom that any chance is a gift, no matter what the cost.

I used to be nervous enough greeting them as they returned from college, new jobs, travel; each had changed a bit since the last time we had been together. When you see those you love infrequently, it takes time to reestablish an honest connection. I liken it to adjusting the level on the stereo, turning the bass and treble knobs in search of perfect harmony.

But greeting their wives unnerves me even more, especially since I have had my inevitable slips with both of them. Each faux pas has made me cautious. As much as I want to be natural with them, my manner invariably becomes forced, and I find myself adjusting to *their* rhythms and ideas.

When I was first introduced to my sons' women, each was on her best behavior. There would be thank-you notes after visits, little gestures of appreciation, gifts even. After thirty years in a household of men, I became entranced by the notion of having women around. But once each was married, a subtle power shift took place; eager openness was replaced by guarded politeness. In each case I sensed competition between us, two women involved with the same man. Fearing the reputation of clingy mother and the sting of all those awful mother-in-law jokes, I distanced myself. But that only exacerbated my feeling that everything had suddenly changed.

"I thought I would be gaining a daughter!" I moaned to my cousin's daughter one day.

"That's unrealistic," she replied. "When I get married, why would I want another mother? I already have one."

Her point was well taken and set me straight. My sons' wives relish their autonomy, even flaunt it, and so I've stopped trying to be anything more than a supporter and am grateful to participate when asked. They make it simple, with their carefully drawn boundaries and well-orchestrated activities. But staying on the periphery of their lives takes some doing for someone who has spent much of her adult life being indispensable and responsible.

I used to probe, wanting to know more than they chose to reveal, until one daughter-in-law stopped me in the game. "You always ask how I feel about this or that," she said firmly but with a convincing smile. "Don't you know feelings aren't thoughts? They're not always something you can talk about or explain. They're just what they are—feelings!" I could only guess that she had arrived at this opinion because she is a dancer and emotes with her body, not words. In any case, I now refrain from either asking them about their feelings or showing mine.

Still, I long to be close to my sons and their wives and

find myself wondering why. My friend Joan tells me it's pretty hard just to drop what you enjoy so much. "That's why you walk on eggshells, trying not to hurt or misjudge," she says.

"True," I agreed, as we talked about my apprehension around this impending reunion weekend. "But I no longer want to edit my behavior, twisting myself up like a pretzel."

"You won't," she assured me. "Now that you've tasted the other, you won't go backwards. It'll be better than ever, you'll see. Just let whatever comes flow through you and then away. Everyone is after the same thing, y'know. It's called intimacy. The only way to experience it is to be yourself."

Anyway, I've hardly had time to fret. Yesterday was my last day of clamming, and I haven't had the energy to do more than tidy up the place. For once, financial pressures and simple existence have taken precedence over self-inflicted anxiety. I did make a bouillabaisse for dinner, full of hand-picked steamers, but I'm counting on everyone to pitch in for the other meals. I shake my head in amusement, thinking back to the ridiculous culinary productions I used to orchestrate, turning the household into a fantasy of impossible perfection, only to end up exhausted and irritable.

I look at the clock. Two hours until they arrive. Oh, God, let me enjoy the pleasure of being graceful! As I gaze about the patio at the flowering perennials that endure year after year, I do myself a favor and recognize that I am no more or less than the perennial that provides the bulk of the lush backdrop for her family and those around her. It has taken years of growing and expanding to become as colorful and abundant as I am. I'm not some hothouse flower, forced into bloom, but rather a ripened woman who is getting to know what she's about. There's no need for me to fret over the young seedlings.

My instinct is to approach the weekend as if I am treading water, keeping my body upright, watching the action, calling on my instincts, remaining centered, not going in one direction or another. I intend to listen more, talk less, receive whatever it is they offer, and then, like the woman I've become, let the ripe fruit fall where it may.

My older son arrives first. He's the traditionalist, the enthusiast, the one who will set a celebratory tone for the weekend, which takes the pressure off me. Our younger son and his wife come next, as if they have choreographed their arrival, appearing during a lull in the action, making it possible for me to welcome them all in measured doses.

The boys greet one another and begin talking as if they had never been apart. I think back to the rehearsal dinner for our older son's wedding, when he lifted his glass and toasted his younger brother, borrowing a sentiment his paternal grandmother held for her sons: "No woman will ever come between me and my brother." I wonder, as the years go on, if he will be able to keep his promise.

Within the hour my husband arrives, and the quiet cottage wakes up, as if from a Rip Van Winkle slumber. This place, which has been used as a retreat for life's richness, can't help but glow with good energy from times well spent: nights of song and games of charades, pine floors permanently tarnished from those who spend days on boats and in sand, late-afternoon homecomings with a line of salty people waiting by the outside shower. There is a central spirit that everyone shares, not unlike the cozy connectedness of a Christmas Eve. It feels right to surrender my isolation. I'm hungrier than I thought for family.

My husband is imbued with an unusually generous spirit, wide watery eyes, hugs for everyone, even me. I automatically pull away from his embrace and then wonder why, since the touch feels good. Practiced repression has no room in my new life, so I slip my arm through his.

The repartee between the boys and their father makes me sense that they have been communicating frequently. There's no doubt the boys bring out his best side. Their affection for him is more readily apparent than their feelings for me, and he responds as anyone would who is being loved. I'm comforted that he hasn't allowed a void to develop between them. Whatever conversations they've been having don't seem to have involved me or the marriage. I surprise myself by feeling relieved.

There are few secrets in a tiny cottage and precious little privacy, yet I'm taken aback when my younger son appears in the kitchen carrying my clam basket and rake. "Who's the clammer? Don't tell me you've taken that up as well," he says, already embarrassed by my job in the fish market.

The others wander in, their curiosity piqued by the conversation. "So that's how you got your tan so soon," says one. "Gee, Mom, what happened? We weren't under the impression that this was one of your lifelong career goals."

"The hot-water heater busted," I confess. "Clamming was a way to get some quick cash."

"But your bad back." One of the girls asks, "How did you manage?"

"The work has actually strengthened my muscles," I answer. "Anyway, you mostly use your upper body."

I am getting the impression that my kids view me as old and finished. They mostly see me in the role of mother, not Joan, the person. Standing here, answering their questions, I feel a certain smugness, triumph actually. I'm proud to be seen as one who pulls her own weight.

My husband, who is leaning against the kitchen sink sipping a glass of wine, has been listening intently with a bemused look on his face. He says nothing, but when he catches my eye, he raises his glass to me.

Slowly, this most ordinary day begins to glow, and the weekend commences. The curtain opens, the drama begins— three whole days, like a three-act play that will never be performed quite the same way again. There is a sense of expectancy in everyone—the daughters-in-law who have never spent a span of time together; the brothers, bonded by blood but changed by transitions; the parents, tainted by separation, strengthened by solitude. Everyone appears hopeful, excited simply by the ritual of the weekend itself. My shyness is further assuaged when a daughter-in-law hands me a gift, a hand-painted sign that says TRADITION. I hang it on the kitchen wall and know that my desire to bring us all together each year is right, that we are intertwined in some indefinable way. Her gesture starts me breathing again, steadily, rhythmically.

* * *

As if the cottage were not enough to bond us together, the weather cooperates by being warm for May and blesses us with a beach day. Not that we couldn't have gotten by with mist and rain, but somehow being out under the big sky with the sensuous sounds of water and wind ensures fun, frolic, and freedom.

"Which beach?" the boys ask, as I am now the native. I choose South Beach, built by a storm, now to be our playground. Big ocean beaches were always my preference when the boys were small, busy, and loud. I counted on the sea to soak up their sounds and wildness.

We pile into the Volvo, my husband motioning for me to climb into the front seat beside him, and it feels like déjà vu, all those years of driving to the beach in a car stuffed with food, drink, Wiffle ball, and bat, and, most of all, an eagerness to get there and stay all day.

We choose the shelter of a dune and unpack our belongings, right next to a colony of sandpipers seemingly unperturbed by our presence. After a time one, then another, lifts off, and each of us, in our own way, follows suit. One of the girls chases a white heron, as a child would a kite, while the other searches for bleached shells. "The more broken the better," she says, "because then you can see right through to the center."

By noon the towels and blankets that have been protecting us from the morning chill come off, and we peel away layers of both clothes and pretension. Manners melt as we fall under the spell of this wild place. The gift of such a day is sinking into a seamless world of uninterrupted time, where the endless hours allow something to grow from nothing.

I watch, as if peering through the lens of a movie camera, shifting from one frame to another. Truths, once held as secrets, slip out. Similarities and differences become comfortable companions in this primitive place where violence and peace go hand in hand.

I overhear my husband confess his anger and lethargy, for which he is getting therapy; a son admits to making a fool of himself at work; the other confesses to a conflict in his marriage. I like watching them share, not just the good stuff but the bad. Men rarely talk to each other as women do. Although my boys are feminists, we raised them to grab the brass ring. By doing so, they are reticent, I fear, to share their hard times, eager only to report the successes, which makes really knowing their grown-up selves all the more difficult.

As a young bride I sent my parents letters filled with lies, wanting to convince not only them, but myself, that I was happy. It occurs to me that I will continue to know my children less if they think I want them to *be* more. Seeking perfection is a terrible thing when it robs you of truth. I wonder if role-playing and being careful are the chief causes of loneliness.

It is only a matter of time before the boys are swimming in the cold spring sea, not because they were once sailors and raised near the water but because one has dared the other. I sit chilled, knowing they are romping about in fifty-degree water and marvel at the glory of their youth, just as my husband takes a running dash and joins them. Minutes later a wave spills all three onto the shore, and the boys rush to roll around on a mound of warm, soft sand. If there had been an ounce of tension left in any of us, it has been banished.

At times like this I find myself wondering how I came to have these particular children. Are they what I expected? Am I totally responsible for what they've become? One is a teacher, the other an actor. I fear for the financial security of the latter and worry that the teacher will get bored in his job. I know I've both spoiled and repressed them, contributed to their neuroses, encouraged their sensitivities, pushed the limits of their goodwill. Yet with all of their foibles, I remain enchanted by their essence, their individual lives, and awfully curious about all I don't know about them, especially their interaction with their wives, who have settled on another mound of sand, sculpting a mermaid. Bent over, digging diligently, they are joined by their men.

My husband and I wander off with the excuse of looking for scallop shells to create the mermaid's fin, but actually we want some time alone. We are two people who have taken steps toward selfhood this year and are in need of sharing what we are becoming.

He seems to be appreciating family as never before; having withdrawn for a time like a hibernating bear, he returns, eager for rediscovery. I find myself walking along a beach with someone who feels like an old friend. We have chosen to walk on firm sand near the surf, where waves splash around us, rinsing the sand from our feet time and again.

I've come to believe that love happens when you want it to. It is an intention, rather than a serendipitous occurrence.

Only when one is open to receive and absorb love can it occur.

"You know, I'm beginning to think that real growing only begins after we've done the adult things we're supposed to do," I say.

"Like what?" he asks.

"Working, raising a family, doing community things— all that stuff keeps you from your real self, the person you've left behind."

"So . . . ?" he asks, waiting for more.

"I don't ever want to be finished. Now that I'm catching on to real living . . . the formlessness of it . . ."

He doesn't understand the concept of unfinished, nor does he see it as a positive word. Part of him wants to be finished, away from his dull job and the need to collect the weekly paycheck. He wants to have that behind him. And yet, what would he be without that definition? This is what he finds scary.

"We're as unfinished as the shoreline upon this beach," I tell him. "Isn't that exciting? Up until now we've done what everyone else wanted us to do, and now it's our turn. I hope to continue to transcend myself as long as I live."

I realize as I speak that my words might be falling on deaf ears. Neither of us has any idea of where we're headed. We've never been as unsure of our future as we are now. And yet, there is a degree of excitement to not knowing, like the young couples we have just left behind. What is clear about their future?

He stops walking now, and I turn to meet his gaze. Tears are streaming down his cheeks. The thawing of a relationship takes hard work. I find it curious that our time is occurring in the spring, when everything else is waking up. It occurs to me that nothing ever really comes to an end. Being by the sea has taught me that.

"Look," I say, breaking the silence, "all I know is that I have spent the bulk of this year unlearning all the rules, the conditions and goals that were set for me by someone else. Finally I feel mature enough to recover myself—that person I was born to be."

He takes my hand, and we walk back to the others, collecting scallop shells as we go. It is one of those walks when, after it is over, you know something has changed.

We see the family, and the flurry of activity that occurs when one must race against the tide to construct a work of art. Just as we are finding various pieces to create the perfect mermaid, so we must dedicate as much time to carefully putting back together the pieces of our own lives. An artist has endless possibilities when the medium is sand and water. So it is also with human sculpture. We are as malleable as the mermaid in the sand—unfinished men and women making new creations out of our old selves.

I relish the passion that bubbles up in this family when we all work together. "Vital lives are about action," Joan Erikson tells me. "You can't feel warmth unless you create it, can't feel delight unless you play, can't know serendipity unless you risk." I'm trying to bring more of the spontaneous beach back to the cottage and incorporate it into my everyday life.

Perhaps the delight I feel right now has to do with the

display of diversity as two generations of men and women evolve, change, and grow. Suddenly the issue of *how* we're all changing seems irrelevant. The fact that we're all striving toward unknown ends is what is so grand. Although I see the essence of my sons, what they become will forever be a surprise. The task is to applaud each surprise as if it were a birthday package plunked in front of me, enjoying the fictional flair of our life stories as they evolve.

The boys are constantly chiding me about my idiosyncrasies. I'm supposedly nosy, loud, inappropriate. You name it, they think it. I, too, see characteristics and attitudes in them and their wives that could stand adjusting. But what makes them interesting are their imperfections. They are perfect in their imperfections! Could that be?

Although the rosy glow of the late afternoon tempts us to linger, the sun will set all too soon, and it is time to gather our belongings. Having arrived at high tide, complete with the ocean's applause, having watched the sea turn itself around during the ebb, and now preparing to leave as the water retreats, I feel full up. To experience the whole of the tide cycle is to view change, to watch time actually pass by. In the process, I feel the pull and tug of the universe.

We don't get dinner on the table until way past nine. I say "we" when in fact the girls take on the duty while I act merely as a sous-chef. One creates a pasta sauce out of several cans of tomato paste, tarragon, and cream, while the other throws together a salad with greens, avocados, grapefruit, and her fabulous raspberry vinaigrette. Preparing a meal together can be like a ballet, as each surrenders to the other's ideas. The fly in the ointment is the woman who insists that certain foods can be only prepared one way—her way. Being reactive instead of proactive is offering me connection.

There is no dessert, the candles are burning low, the last bottle of wine is being opened, great yawns are replacing vivid conversation. Someone once said that a good husband is the workmanship of a good mother. So, for the moment, I take credit for how the boys have turned out, especially in their earnest endeavors at husbandhood.

If I had longed for felt satisfaction back at Christmastime, I am finally experiencing it. Gathering around a table, breaking bread together, offers those who partake a piece of something sacred. For now I am briefly liberated by the simple act of living. I watch the sideways glances the young couples indulge in as one thing or another is said and enjoy their ample displays of affection. I used to be envious of young love, but tonight I delight in its warmth.

And then my husband stands to deliver a toast:

"Here's to our wives and sweethearts.
May our sweethearts soon be our wives,
and our wives always our sweethearts."

I listen with my heart, reminded that some of my sons' behavior had to have been modeled after their father.

14

SAFE HARBOR

End of June

If it is woman's function to give, she must be replenished too.

—*Anne Morrow Lindbergh,* GIFT FROM THE SEA

It is early morning, soggy with high humidity, the kind of weather that defies lightness. Even so, I spring to my feet at the sound of the chirping birds and tiptoe down to the kitchen to prepare a Thermos of coffee. My older son and his wife leave today, having stayed long after the others to spend some quality time with me before departing on a Far Eastern bike trip.

Their sleepy heads appear just before dawn, and I walk them to their overstuffed little Dodge, bikes strapped to the roof, and hug them hard, holding on to my son for an extra moment. Then, like the ship captain's wife, I wave good-bye, a brave smile on my face and a lump in my throat. It's not that I want to hold on to them. It's just that I've not fully faced the inevitability of children's growing up and going so far away. I tend to linger around final moments, hoping to create an indelible impression, not only of what the experience looked like but of what it felt like as well. Endings have a way of plunging me into emotional wilderness, but not this time.

There are fewer tears now, perhaps because I'm beginning to realize they are not mine. They belong to each other; their "own little nation," I say, envisioning them huddled in their tent near some rice paddy. They hold the power of their destinies in their own hands. I can only offer Godspeed. It's a bittersweet reality, but I'm coming to understand that love blossoms when there is just the right amount of tenderness combined with a long leash.

It was good to have them home, but I'm surprised at how anxious I am to regain my solitude. For all the frivolity during our time together, you can't sustain celebration. Nor would I want to, since such joy and fun never come without effort. Although I didn't intend to edit my behavior, I did, nevertheless, minding my manners, holding my tongue, refraining from judgments.

Still, I feel a void, not because everyone is gone but because they are returning to lives that have well-worked-out agendas. It was strange bidding my husband good-bye, too, as if he were only going on a business trip, when, in reality, he was returning to his separate world, although he mentioned retirement more than once, liberally sprinkling his conversations with references to "we" and "us." Since we seemed to be reconnecting, I hesitated to spoil the momentary closeness with questions about the future. But there was something missing, evidence of distance that couldn't be denied.

I wonder now if it had something to do with not having sex. Not that I had necessarily wanted to make love, but I was troubled that it didn't even seem to be an option. I've been obsessed with sexual thoughts lately, longing for that part of my life to be restored, wincing at the sight of love scenes in movies, turning away when I see lovers embracing. I even found myself wondering what was going on between my sons and their wives behind closed doors each night.

Yet in truth, sex has never been high on my list of priorities. Thinking I want something is quite different from actually enjoying it. The myth around sex in this culture is that we should want it, that we are abnormal or repressed if we don't have it, so not partaking of it makes me feel like an outsider.

Perhaps I stopped being available for lovemaking simply because I didn't like it. It seemed fine for helping to pin down a man for marriage, even finer when I wanted children. Then it became a chore—a duty to perform after the dishes were done and the kids were put to bed. Pleasuring her man was what I had been taught a good wife simply should do.

Now, what seems hundreds of years later, I stand here wondering what I've missed. Many of my friends confide that they, too, are relieved that the need to do the "chore" is past. One quit sex because her husband failed to personalize it; for him it seemed any keyhole would do. Another couldn't bear her husband's snorting and sniffing. Another grew bored with her husband's idea of romance: lying in bed reading the swimsuit edition of *Sports Illustrated* while fondling himself, expecting her to become aroused by watching.

Sooner or later, grief and guilt over not having sex drive me to distraction. Why don't I let my ice-cube heart thaw and just get on with it? The worst that could happen is that it might be like before. Yet now that I've managed to reclaim some of my primitive self, who knows? What if, for once, I allowed my body to feel the passion my mind does? Or if, like the Chinese, I began to consider regular sex as paramount to good health and longevity? Would those be reason enough to consummate my longing?

Oh, well, no point to these speculations when there's no

one to make love to anyway. Perhaps just facing up to such unvarnished facts is a step toward a solution.

Today happens to be the summer solstice, a meaningful time for change, and with more daylight than I will see for another year, I'd best seize the hours with a vengeance.

Nearby is my bicycle with its bulbous tires and rusting chain, a workhorse of a vehicle that takes me on jaunts for mail and groceries. Perhaps a longer ride will still my mind and break up my melancholia. I will make it a symbolic journey, the farther the better, in honor of my children's longer one.

I take off through the woods, down our dirt path, and eventually onto pavement. I remember as a little girl heading off without ever having a destination—wonder-filled, expectant, hair flying just as now. My bike leads me, becoming an extension of my body, taking me back.

I am headed down Lovers Lane, now overgrown with wild pink roses and cornflowers. A meadow nearby is awash in purple clover. Gradually, all the colors, aromas, shadows, dips, and pockets become a blur that invites discovery. I'm on a two-lane, sparsely traveled road that cuts across the Cape. It's taking me inland, away from the beach traffic, past cranberry bogs, kettle ponds, and scrub-pine forests. Just now I understand why my daughter-in-law prefers bikes over other vehicles: "You miss nothing when you're moving two miles an hour," she says. "Even the smallest blade of grass can capture your attention." Just now it is the smell of bayberry, honeysuckle, and pine that captures mine.

My tongue touches my salty upper lip. I'm surprised at

how good the sweat tastes. All this moving, stretching, and breathing align my thoughts with my body's feelings. I wonder if I could share a long bike ride with my husband. What would happen if we had to depend on one another the way our son and his wife are about to do? We did once, when we were first married and living in Africa. Maybe we've lasted this long because we learned to be interdependent back then.

I stop thinking and pedal harder to make a hill. At the top I take my feet off the pedals, abandon all control, and race down the other side, skidding at the bottom on a sandy shoulder and braking in front of the Methodist Church, where a sign proclaims: THE OPPOSITE OF LOVE IS INDIFFERENCE. The message is haunting, even wounds me. I get off my bike and plop down onto the lawn, still moist and sweet-smelling from the early-morning dew. Sweat tickles my back as the drops, one by one, slide between my shoulder blades, I reach for my water bottle to take a couple of gulps before pulling my knees up to my chin and rocking out a kink in my back. I am still in recovery from the hour or so of hard riding, but I turn to the sign once more to muse over the word "indifference."

Had I become indifferent to my husband and marriage? I hate the thought. It denotes not caring, having little feeling, being cold and harsh. Am I that? I hope not. Perhaps we were simply tired souls who hadn't the energy for anything but inertia, both shutting down and keeping our feelings to ourselves.

But we were anything but indifferent to one another over Memorial Day, sharing easy conversation, exchanging knowing glances, seeing humor in our lives. Maybe separating was the sanest thing for two confused people to do, coming coincidentally as it did at menopause—hmmm, men-o-pause, a pause from men. Perhaps all women in long-term relationships should consider it. Primitive cultures insist on it, knowing a woman needs to regenerate, not unlike the starfish growing a new arm or the molting lobster growing larger and stronger within a new shell.

If I'm obsessing over indifference, it must mean I still care. Perhaps at one time I was indifferent, but no more, not about him or the marriage or any other aspect of my life. It's not that I don't ever want him to return home. It's just that I want it only if it is intentional, not a mere matter of convenience. If we are to have a future, it must be a collaboration, where each has a hand in the plot and contributes to the stage directions. I no longer have any interest in producing and directing the third act of our lives.

The carillon in the church steeple breaks my concentration with its melodious midmorning concert, a familiar tune:

> *"Morning has broken, like the first morning,*
> *Blackbird has spoken, like the first bird.*
> *Praise for the singing, praise for the morning,*
> *Praise for them springing, fresh from the word."*

I sing along, uplifted by the words, reminded of the way my favorite minister taught me how to pray, or rather, yield my thoughts: "Offer praise first," she said, "then thanksgiving. Follow it with petition, asking for your need to be met, and then conclude by relinquishing control." I find that once I do the first part, the reason for my prayer usually diminishes.

The little concert concludes when the bell in the church tower strikes ten. The day is young, and I have rebounded from a sense of loss to feeling as new as the morning.

What to do next? With no one around and no need to take a consensus, the sky's the limit. I hop back on my bike and head for the bike path, which takes me away from the tourist traffic and deeper into the interior of the Cape. Nostalgia works as a magnet and draws me five miles north to my reward—a general store that has been around as long as I can remember. Shoving my bike into a crowded bike stand, I hobble toward the front porch, where the same men who sit around the store's potbellied stove in the winter now sit on old church pews outside, drinking from bottomless cups of coffee, watching the world go by, and catching up on each other's business.

Once inside, I sit on a milk carton beside the newspapers, which are directly under the revolving ceiling fan. The breeze and the distraction of two little kids eyeing the penny candy and jars full of affordable toys make me forget that I am hot and sweaty. You can get your mail here, buy postage stamps, read the notices of upcoming events, pick up fruits, vegetables, freshly ground peanut butter, spices sold by the ounce, canned jelly made by a local housewife, homemade breads and muffins made by another, and general supplies such as lantern oil, sturdy pottery, and other staples necessary for a household. They carry one brand of most everything, not twenty, making it simple to choose. Nothing is complicated or fancy here, just practical and friendly. This is a place to linger, a microcosm of a small town; in fact, the general store *is* the town, that and several churches on nearby corners. I'm thinking, as I sit here and drink in the scene, how little it takes to get by, how simple life really can be, how pleasant to think only of necessities, eliminating the luxuries. Just now I recognize that this is everything I want—this is home. The Cape is where I belong, where I must stay. The kids may go far and wide and my husband may have other ideas, but as for me, this is contentment.

After buying a lemonade I'm ready for the return trip home, pedaling easily this time, in no particular hurry. Wind chimes, a gift from my children, greet me upon my return, along with a sinkful of last night's dirty dishes, soiled towels piled high in the back hall, and several workmen up on my roof!

"Hey, what are you guys doing up there?"

"Fixing a leak and then replacing half the shingles," one of them answers, as if he is puzzled by the question.

"Are you sure you have the right house?" I ask. "I didn't order any work to be done."

"Yeah, well your husband did . . . called us a couple of weeks back. After this job we're supposed to insulate the attic and paint the trim."

Totally mystified now, I go to the phone and dial his number. "What's up with the workmen on the roof?" I ask my husband, barely saying hello.

"Oh, good," he answers. "I'm glad they showed up. They weren't sure when they'd be able to work us in."

"Work us in! What's going on?"

"I thought you'd be pleased," he says, surprised at the edginess in my voice.

"Well, I guess I am, but you could have warned me. Besides, your interest in this house is a huge turnaround from the water-heater incident. What gives?"

"We've got to preserve the cottage," he says. "It means so much to everyone, even the kids."

The conviction with which he is speaking has obvious underpinnings. Then he mumbles something about wanting to reinvest in us.

I'm not sure I like what I'm hearing, but nonetheless, here it is. He's contemplating returning, living here, being with me. In a daze, I fill him in on our son's departure and then say good-bye. For a moment or two I stand with the phone still in my hand. My mind races with questions. When is he thinking of returning? What is he planning to do here? What does he think it will take for us both to create a life here—to re-create one together? What do I really want? But then, all of a sudden, I find myself not wanting to know anymore. For now the cottage is being restored and that's enough, especially since I've only just decided that this is where I intend to stay. It's been a long day. For now I want to retain my praise for this grand solstice day, and let the future evolve as it will.

15

WILD AND SALTY

August

If you can risk getting lost somewhere along the day you might
stumble upon openings that link you to your depths.

—*Anonymous*

I *have* learned to pay attention to my instincts and take notice when I feel anxious—to remove the pebble from my shoe before it blisters, get the chicken bone out of my throat—in short, to be mindful of feelings and emotions and work with them, not run from them. Such is the reason I find myself on this early Tuesday morning being ferried by boat to the outer bar, where I will stay overnight, going off alone before being joined by another.

There is no doubt I was startled by my husband's talk of retirement and reconciliation. Having spent the past year shuttling between married woman and free spirit, I thought it prudent to take stock of my wishes and desires before yielding to something I hadn't bargained for. Taking a wild and salty cure by spending twenty-four hours on a rugged spit of land seemed the perfect tonic for my free-floating anxiety: a place where I would stay present, buoy my spiritual armor, and return satisfied that my hard-won autonomy was intact.

The boat moves swiftly now. I grip my trusty old sleeping bag and backpack, remnants from more difficult experiences: trekking the Andes and hiking to the bottom of the Grand Canyon, both gratifying adventures that tested my will and stamina but, because I went with others, failed to test my independence. This adventure isn't as dramatic and is certainly not about miles hiked or mountaintops scaled, but as I will be completely alone with nature, I do expect it to be a deepening experience.

The twenty-minute trip passes quickly, and we soon pull into a little cove where disembarking looks manageable. I negotiate my way over the side of the boat, wade ashore carrying tent and sleeping bag, then return for food, water, and other supplies.

"See ya tomorrow, late morning," the captain says, backing his boat away, then adding an ominous note: "Remember, middle-of-the-night rescues are not part of my package. Hope the weather holds." With that, he's off, and the sound of his motor fades, removing the last din of everyday life.

I stand still, feet sinking into the muddy flat, and experience a familiar fear, nothing extreme, just a gnawing concern that comes over me when first I'm left alone in any situation, particularly one I have stubbornly seized upon despite warnings from well-meaning friends.

"Aren't you afraid something will happen to you?" a neighbor asked upon seeing me pack the trunk of my car.

"I certainly hope so," I answered defensively. "That's the whole point."

Pity that life teaches us to be so careful and guarded, I thought, as I drove away, but now, looking around at this utter wildness, I wonder if she knows something I don't. For sure, the weather is supposed to turn—it is hurricane season, after all—but not for another forty-eight hours. I've been forced into this window of time because of these predictions, but I also want to take advantage of the full moon.

A series of gentle waves washes over the tips of my

rubber boots, signaling not only a turning tide but my immediate task—getting my gear to higher ground. I spot a gawky piece of driftwood, bare limbs sticking out all over, and prop my stuff at its base. Then I survey this serene setting and the 360-degree view it affords. I adjust my breath to the ocean's rumble, which at the moment is calm and unperturbed, and set out to find a campsite. As I trudge up one dune and down another, I am hampered by my boots in the soft sand, but the combination works its magic and puts my high-gear personality into slow motion.

My eye is drawn to one scooped-out hollow, then another, until I choose a completely bald spot with no new sprouts of dune grass in its basin and three sides of protective, towering mounds, a perfect spot in which to nestle my dome tent.

In little over an hour my nesting place is set up. I've gone from panic to peace—anxiety falling away, along with a headache, muscles becoming mush, brain draining of all complicated thought. Taking to a nearby perch with a natural seat carved into the side of a dune, I'm further tranquilized by the sounds of lapping water and wind.

Just beneath where I sit is a remarkable sight: a perfectly drawn circle in the smooth sand, created by one blade of swaying beach grass being moved by the wind. It is just as if someone had taken a draftman's compass to draw a radius. Fledgling beach grass is a marvel. I can only imagine how difficult it was for it to become so deeply rooted, so much of its growth hidden, a survivor of storms, shifting sands, and wild seas. Perhaps this is meant to be a sign for me, maybe even of the marriage in which I have come full circle, engaging my senses like so many tufts of beach grass to bring me to the center of myself. I feel as still and sure as the axis of a wheel, both in and out of relationship, wishing no longer to meddle with the workings of fate but to remain in the hub while the elements do the work.

Powerful messages are available in a place where strife is more common than peace, where impermanence reigns and all that lives is subject to change and erasure. I feel a kinship with this environment as I, too, have made *change* my friend.

I'm eager to walk, stretch, explore this paradise set in a circle of waves, to get to know her times and moods. Starting out on the protected side of the bar, I saunter along the edges of the shore, where the beach tapers and rough seas mingle with a tame bay. My feet must negotiate with the ever-increasing tide that washes over my footprints almost as quickly as I create them. I like the idea of taking sanctuary in a place where one's movements become an unsolvable mystery, with no clues left behind.

The idea of slipping away without explanation and having secrets has become a staple of my year by the sea. Soon I will be obliged to explain my daily routines to another. "I shall miss having secrets," I told Joan recently.

"Ah, but you must always retain some part of yourself which is nobody's business. The minute you let others in on your secrets, you've given away some of your strength."

Here, where much more is hidden than apparent, I am reminded that a companion to mystery is peace; that knowing less and wondering more offers expectancy. It has become my way to dispense with incessant seeking in favor of stumbling upon answers. In the words of Picasso, "I find, I do not seek." No longer desperate to know every outcome, these days I tend to wait and see, a far more satisfying way of being that lacks specificity and instead favors experience over analysis.

I plow on, sensing that someone is following me, a silly thought out here, but nonetheless I feel something lurking. The only creature that could possibly follow me is a fox or coyote, both of which hide from people, not stalk them. Still, I hear weird noises, even feel some vibrations, and after a few minutes see what I already felt, not on land but in the water. A parade of seals, temporarily washed off their sand-bar, have taken to the water for their daily exercise, swimming beside me as I walk, playing hide-and-seek until just now, when one makes eye contact with me, and I stop to hold its gaze.

"Hi there," I say, a broad smile splashing across my face as I talk to the air, attempting to carry on a conversation with the seals as my voice keeps them watching. "You guys have gotten me to do all kinds of crazy things since the first time we met," I say. "I've actually become a little mad."

With that, they all dive, then surface some fifty yards away, looking back at me as if to say, "C'mon."

I pick up my pace, fully engaged with their company, now honored by it, and find myself skipping, moving in sync with their arching dives, responding to their raw impulses. I catch myself believing the Celtic myth that in the dark pool of a seal's eyes there are spirits that call out to certain people.

No doubt the seals touched me back in October, urging me with their antics to be more playful, vulnerable, and free, insisting that I begin to look at what was missing in my life. Just now I am overcome by the reality that they did set me on a new path, that they have made a difference. Tears stain my cheeks, further reminding me how keenly alive I am just now.

We are nearing the tip of the island, where bay and ocean collide and water gushes. Waves ripple on either side of the point, careening, crashing, splashing, creating convoluted channels. The heaving surf is just beyond, now hissing through gleaming stones that are deposited upon the shore, and I stare at the sheer marvel of their survival, imagining the great mountain of which they were once a part, aware of their evolution from land to sea floor to shore.

I sit and grab handfuls of sand, letting the grains flow through my fingers, seeing in them my limitless future, a stark contrast from a few months ago when I was bored, counting the hours, staring into an hourglass that measured life in terms of a more prescribed amount of time. I am no longer just passing through the world, but digging deep and collecting moments. Time is a funny thing. Now that I am engrossed in life there is never enough time, but that was before I learned to stretch a moment to an hour and create multiple highs along the expanse of a day. I never saw the possibilities and promises that twenty-four hours actually offer.

The frothy whitecaps appear as a ruffled chorus line dancing across the surface of the sea, spitting, hissing, kicking all the way, acting very much like the woman I'm becoming, not content unless I'm tickling the rocks, slithering up the shore, embracing everything in sight. Catch the ocean as the tide rises and you find yourself amid a force that gets its strength from ebb and flow, that teaches the worth of filling up and emptying.

This afternoon's tide offers a pentimento of abstract patterns, garnished with shells, stones, and debris. The beach has become a canvas upon which an artist has created a collage, only to change his mind before the paint dries and compose a new overlapping image with the advent of the next wave. I, too, over the years have layered my basic frame, adapting to the demands of a culture, the ideals of a mother, designing and redesigning my persona, and now am finally scraping off the excess to have a glimpse of the original self.

I am so fortunate to have a friend like Joan who applauds my progress from the sidelines, helping me to see that whatever stage I'm in should be my project—that receiving and responding are true "tidal behavior," that whatever washes ashore should be greeted, picked up, sifted through, and held on to. As I contemplate living with another again, I must be ready to accept our differences and celebrate our similarities, to watch our new selves emerge and delight in what appears on my "shore."

Acceptance seems the biggest stretch that newly independent people must extend to one another. It is a strength I must acquire, or risk being estranged from the ebb and flow of the rest of my life. Like the tides that come and go at *their* will, not *ours*, we who frequent the beach must be mindful to time our swims and walks to the ocean's law. So it should be with the people who move in and through our lives.

Quickly this warm day is becoming a cool evening. It's time to head back to my temporary shelter, to collect driftwood on the way for tonight's fire. I feel a touch of hesitation as I turn my back and leave the passion of the pounding surf for calmer ground, even though I know that one cannot live on strong emotion alone. I head across the central corridor of my island, the only place that displays any sign of permanence, and where I will probably have the best chance of finding dry wood. It takes some doing for my eyes to adjust to the braided streams of light and shadow before I begin spotting random twigs, weathered boards, small logs half buried beneath silver dune grass and beige sand. My task is made easier when I come upon a twisted wreckage of storm fencing, which offers ample kindling for multiple fires. With arms weighted down, I stumble toward my little camp, happy to dump my load, collapse on my perch with cheese and a glass of wine, and watch day turn to night.

It was smart to bring mostly prepared foods—barbecued chicken, raw vegetables, bread. What's worth cooking if it means missing the sunset? I have never really taken time to truly watch the light show offered by the sun as it sets or the night as it develops. The sun, just disappearing, has left a painted sky of golds, pinks, oranges, and purples before becoming a melancholy blue, then turning to deeper tones of dusk. All is ripely quiet, and I lift my glass to me, a woman turned inside out, no longer wanting to become happy because, finally, I am.

My first impulse is to scavenge in my backpack for a flashlight so that I can read, write in my journal, record what I am experiencing. But then I see the moon turn on its soft white light, and I give over to the novelty of natural light, dropping my dependence on sight for the evening in favor of some of my other senses, as Joan's voice taps in to my consciousness: "The way to keep your senses alive is to use them."

Just then comes the background music of slurping surf, gull wings, and the snapping and crackle of burning wood.

I pull my knees to my chest, wrap my arms around my shins, and drink in the sweet, pungent aroma of driftwood as the sun, salt, and sea are burned from it. The wind creates a fickle flame that darts this way and that like fireflies. I'm hypnotized by the blaze, seeing the burn of struggle, the dance of aliveness, and knowing that the fire bears watching. I do not ever want the passion of my new ways to cool. The nourishment I feel can only be maintained if I stay close to the elements—fire, air, water, earth. If I surround myself with them, I shall always feel the stirrings of my soul.

With the night so luminous, not an inch of sky unused, I hesitate to turn in, wanting to luxuriate under the sequined heavens. I wrap myself in my sleeping bag and lie down, melting into the soft sand, while the ocean's murmur comforts me like a mother. Hours later I'm awakened by a chilling wind, forced to retreat inside my little tent like a snail into its moon shell.

The brightness of the morning stuns me. It seems as if I were only just basking in the moonlight. I've no idea what time it is, having left my watch on the mainland. Gathering clues from the chattering birds and the orange sun about to emerge, I would guess five-thirty. I crawl from the tent and quickly start a fire. As I wait for the water to boil, I huddle close by, in hopes of drying the damp night out of my clothes. Soon I am taking my first glorious sip of hot coffee, as the seals fish for their breakfast and the gulls wait for any scrap of food I'm willing to toss in their direction.

I am utterly content, tranquil in my aloneness, serene. Joan once told me that the root word in Greek for "alone" means "all one." That is precisely what I am experiencing, a sense of that sort of wholeness. Added to the peace of this morning is a quiet low-tide bay that boasts in its center a sandbar that has appeared three times in the past twenty-four hours. It teases me to venture out. I hesitate at first, the thought of chilly water making me shiver, but then, once again, I hear the words of my Navajo elder: "Listen to the muse when it's talking to you or it just goes on, and you miss its statement—that moment when you could have done something."

I put my coffee mug on the sand, strip to underpants and T-shirt, and wade in, searching the shallows for high ground, managing to stay ankle deep for a while. My eyes soon deceive me, and I sink to my thighs. No matter. At the very worst I'll be forced to swim. Intent now upon seeing what this momentary oasis offers, I push on, thighs moving the water aside, until at last I climb up on the sandbar, its surface a treasure trove of starfish and sand dollars, sea life that speaks of regeneration and eternity. I meander far out into the middle of the bay, dreaming about possibility, drinking in the moment, absorbing the grace of this temporary world that allows me to experience what it means to be timebound. You have to hit such a place at just the right moment or risk missing it altogether, for as soon as the sandbar appears, it begins to disappear again.

Standing on this island, I feel the perpetual motion of things—the tides, birds, seals, fish, shoreline, even myself. It seems to me that the task of the unfinished woman is to acknowledge her life as a work in progress, allowing each passage, evolution, experience to offer wisdom for her soul.

As I finally turn back to walk to the other end of the bar, I see that water has already covered up half of it. There is no choice now but to swim to shore. I take off my underpants and T-shirt, with its bold slogan, THIS IS WHAT 50 LOOKS LIKE, and unceremoniously fling them on the bar to be left behind. I dive in and glide as far as my breath will take me.

Stripped bare, I can truly relate to the water as it embraces my flesh. I flip onto my back and surrender myself to the currents as a school of silvery minnows flits over and under me. It feels good to be in my body without all the usual armor. I slide my hands down my sides, swaying in the gentle tide, held as if between the covers on a bed, a primal moment that allows me to see beyond my limits. Momentarily carried away by my fantasies, I don't notice that the current is moving swiftly now, pulling me away from shore. I revert to the side stroke, swimming quickly but remaining relaxed. As one thigh rubs against another, I feel a new confidence in my body, stroke by stroke.

Perhaps being sensual and sexual is nothing more than an attitude toward life. Could it be that the process of unfolding eludes many of us because, as my favorite writer, Nancy Mairs says, "most women carry their genitals as if they are in a sealed envelope." Maybe it's not for a man to open us; instead, we're meant to open ourselves and then relish what follows, with or without a man. It's about time I break my reliance on romance anyhow. As if to punctuate my thoughts, one wave slaps me, then another, as the ocean gathers me up and rolls me closer and closer to shore.

I emerge from the rigors of my swim, naked and unselfconscious, standing on the shore where the sun drys my body and offers color to my breasts, which have never seen the light of day. I feel like Aphrodite, whose lust for living and delight in the sensuous became the core of her being. "Take your dream by the hand and swim with it," Joan keeps telling me. "Let it float."

I see in the distance what must be my T-shirt drifting away, and with it all limitations created by ages and stages. Halfway to a hundred, I feel invincible, ready for new life. I walk back to my camp and step into my shorts and sweatshirt, glad that I thought to pack up my gear beforehand in order to be able to muse through the morning.

With a sudden string of ominous black clouds hanging over the sea and the wind picking up, it is as if on cue that I hear the motor of a boat in the distance.

I lug my gear to the cove and hop aboard, feeling part mermaid, part seal, knowing that something eternal has happened; that my truth depends on regular forays into the wilderness. I make a silent promise always to remember to strive toward the unimaginable.

We pass several seals, bottling just now, and I give them a wave of thanks for helping me reclaim my basic existence. Simple things will keep it so. I must live a little each day, greet the sun as it rises and revel in its setting, swim naked, sip coffee and wine by the shore, generate new ideas, admire myself, talk to animals, meditate, laugh, risk adventures. I must try to be soft, not hard; fluid, not rigid; tender, not cold; find rather than seek. I have been embraced by the sea, tested by its elements, emptied of anxiety, cleansed with fresh thought. In the process, I have recovered myself.

Embracing a husband and reinstating a relationship should be a piece of cake.

16

PORT OF CALL

September

When one has lived a long time alone,
one wants to live again among men and women,
to return to that place where one's ties with the human
broke, where the disquiet of death and now also
of history glimmers its firelight on faces . . .

—*Galway Kinnell, "When One Has Lived*
a Long Time Alone"

Labor Day at the fish market feels like Grand Central Station at rush hour. Summer people wander in and out all day long to pick up boxes of packed-for-travel lobster, scallops, swordfish, so they can take a taste of the Cape back to wherever they come from. Their faces display gloom, as no one wants to turn his back on summer. Some linger to talk about their fall plans, others have no time to talk, already in their harried, hurried mode, and then there are the few who are curious about what happens to us—the locals—after they leave.

"What's it like year-round?" one asks as I slap her cod onto a bed of ice, tucking bluefish pâatè in the corners of the box.

"It's quiet, that's for sure, but there's lots to do," I answer.

"Like what?" she presses, as if trying to believe that her suburban life is far better than life here.

"Empty beaches and bike paths, no lines at restaurants, stuff going on at the museums and libraries. It can even get hectic, if that's your pleasure."

She leaves with a wary look on her face as I wipe down the counters, quietly pleased that I didn't say too much, wanting to keep the joys of winter here a secret, lest we be invaded.

"I'm putting a sword steak in the cooler for you," the

owner says to me, displaying a beautiful cut on the palm of his hand. "Thought you might want to welcome your hubby home in grand style."

I'm taken aback. He doesn't often give his fish away, certainly not sword at $12.95 a pound. "Look forward to meeting him," he adds, "just to see if it's true, you having a husband and all that."

Time flies, this being the market's busiest day, save the Fourth of July. I leave at slack time, around two, and follow a caravan of cars home, rooftops covered with gear, bicycles hanging from their racks, boats being hauled to marinas for winter storage, all signs that summer is over.

My past Labor Days were fraught with much of the same bittersweet activity—stripping the beds, beating sand out of the hooked rugs, emptying the refrigerator, loading the car, always trying to accomplish the chores in record time so I could have one last walk on the beach. No longer. While everyone departs, I now simply wave good-bye. At long last, this day has lost its poignancy.

Yesterday I planted a hundred tulip bulbs, not because I'm suddenly interested in gardening but out of anticipation, knowing I'll be able to watch them bloom in April—that and to remind myself that I shall always be that enduring, blooming perennial I woke up to a few months back.

I hop into the outside shower as soon as I get home, rinsing off the smell of the fish market, wrap myself in an over-sized beach towel, and settle onto a chaise longue with a book and glass of iced tea, wanting to take advantage of the last few hours of single life. My husband will be arriving at six. I'm planning to meet him at a local watering hole. I've invited a variety of people there to drink to his future, dubbing the event a change-of-life party, wishing to ritualize his stepping over the threshold into this new life. Perhaps he'll be appalled at such an event, perhaps not. I figure this will be only the first of many surprises for both of us.

I doze for a bit, the sun both warming and relaxing my body, then pick some of my neighbors' Shasta daisies offered to me as they left this morning. I put them in a vase and then gaze around at the cottage, recalling what a comfortable refuge this has been for me this past year. Everything remains the same, except I've created a room of my own off the kitchen, with windows facing the woods, my only statement (to myself actually) that I must remain my own person. I've had the notion ever since a therapist friend showed me her sparsely furnished tower room with a view of the Hudson River. "I permit only objects and people of my choosing here," she said, "wanting pure space, with no negative energy, just for myself."

I feel a tad nervous as the day winds down—nothing serious, just the queasiness one feels before a first day of school or showing up for a new job. I step into my dress-up uniform—blue jeans and black linen blazer—comb my tousled hair, apply fresh lipstick, dab lemon-scented perfume behind my ears, and tell myself to calm down. You don't look half bad, I think as I peer into the mirror. A leathery tan accentuates my wrinkles, but the overall effect is handsome and hearty, a salty lady full of grit, sensitivity, and earthiness.

Once behind the wheel of the car, with a wad of my own hard-earned money in my pocket to pay for this little party, I open all the windows and let the wind blow in its unique freshness, then replay my husband's last phone call, when his voice sounded uncharacteristically up. No doubt he's done some work on himself—therapy, a few retreats, even yoga. He now has the voice of someone who has reinvoked his own passion. I'm anticipating greeting an unfinished man, a good soul, and an old friend, all the while knowing that my future and his remain a mystery still to be unraveled.

Main Street is dead, emptied of cars, summer obviously over. Now is the time when you recognize people in stores, take more than a moment to have a chat with them. Once at the restaurant I find a parking space right in front and go in, surprised to see so many of my guests already there: several fish-market employees, a woman photographer I hope to work with, the postmistress, two year-round couples I've gotten to know, Joan Erikson, and Josh Cahoon. Still to arrive are my plumber and his wife, two neighbors, and, of course, my husband.

The bartender has put out a tray of veggies and dip, "compliments of the house," he informs me. I indulge in light chatter while keeping one eye on the door and one on the clock—it's six-thirty. He must be stuck in holiday traffic.

Two glasses of wine later, the man of the hour appears, as if in a mirage, a little road-weary but excited just the same. After a lingering embrace that gives him a moment to adjust to the surprise, I introduce him to the unfamiliar faces and then retreat to the side to watch this six-foot-four-inch man relax into the spirit of the evening. His palpable presence warms my heart, as I remember how often he used to turn away from people—from the effort and intimacy involved—but not tonight. One of the guests, another retired man, approaches him with scissors in hand and ceremoniously cuts off his tie. Everyone cheers as my husband twirls it around as if it were a lasso and flings it to the rafters. I move closer and make a toast to his change of life, giving him a tide clock instead of the proverbial watch men are so often given at retirement.

We have endured, it would seem. A year ago in anger and despair I would have eagerly reached for divorce. But lethargy and exhaustion prevailed. Separation and solitude have healed us. It wasn't the marriage that needed to be terminated, rather the rote way in which we were existing within its walls.

There will be unknown jolts and instabilities as we live for a time on an unmoored raft, our days and ways as unstable perhaps as they were in adolescence. Fortunately, I no longer crave ease in life; that exquisite idleness so many people long for seems stifling to me now. I'm much more eager to delight in the ridiculous, just as we are doing at this moment.

In any case, the next few months will surely not be stolid or settled, and I've promised not to instruct or ask my husband what he is going to do with the rest of his life. I detest seeing wives ordering their husbands about, prematurely turning them into sniveling old men. I'll listen to his thoughts and ideas but hesitate before offering opinions. No one needs to be taught at this stage of life; rather, our own senses and sensitivities should carve out our paths. Falling into old patterns would only serve to diminish our spiritual growth.

In time the crowd dwindles, and we take a seat at a corner table to order some dinner. He wants his favorite, fried clams; I choose oysters on the half shell, after which he insists we share a split of champagne, our custom when having oysters.

"Baby, what a surprise!" he says of the party, melting me with my father's endearment, something he does from time to time now that my father is gone. "But how much did that cost?"

A typical question from a newly retired man who is unsure about his financial future, I think.

"It was *my* party," I answer, "paid for with fish-market earnings and an unexpected royalty check. Besides, your decision to change your life is a big deal. Haven't we always marked such events? Certainly the kids have had their fair share of parties. It's the least I could do."

He looks pleased and content. The afterglow of years permits us to be quiet together. Just as I feel a sense of peacefulness settling across the table, he interrupts the moment. "Remember how mad you got when I announced a few years back that I was at peace with myself?"

"How could I forget? Since I wasn't feeling peaceful, all I could think was, Why should you?"

"Right," he continued. "Of course, I didn't know what the hell I was talking about. I suppose I thought if I named the state of mind I was wishing for, it might come to pass. Well, guess what? Being at peace with oneself means being without passion, and that's what I've been missing—not just the sex stuff but the old adrenaline rush that comes when you're doing something crazy. Being stubborn and staid hasn't done much for me. I need to go back to the prescription I gave our marriage at the beginning—that we should always have adventures, both together and independent of each other."

"I'm coming to see that life is not a lesser thing than I imagined it to be," I say, thinking out loud just now. "Rather, it holds more than I have time to seize. The big secret is that everything doesn't happen in youth."

He nods. It occurs to me that the time for parting is past. If one or the other of us were going to jump ship, it would have had to happen before the kids were married, before the circle and tribe began enlarging and we began to see the potential for regeneration. I suppose there never was a good reason for us not to be together.

Separation has done its job—less of him has made more of me and vice versa. Funny how I focused on the sex issue, as if that should stop us from living together. A marriage has to have some flaws, some unresolved issues, some conflicts that can be worked through. Hopefully long-term marriages move beyond chemistry to compatibility anyway.

A moment of truth always brings with it an intensity that is delicious. Right now my cheeks have turned a deep pink as I return to a solid state of gratitude. If we both live consciously into each day, I'm convinced now that the most ordinary of our experiences will glow with meaning.

I am yawning with weariness as we pay the bill and begin to leave. "I have an idea for tomorrow," my husband says.

"Tomorrow," I say, startled. Thinking beyond right now is a jolt.

"Would you take me to see the seals?" he asks. "I want to

see why they mean so much to you. Perhaps they'll even speak to me."

"No doubt they will," I answer.

Like me, he is on a new path. I can only sit by and honor what is unfinished in him—in all of us.

A Year by the Sea

Joan Anderson

ABOUT THE BOOK

Life is a work in progress, as ever-changing as a sandy shore-line. *A Year by the Sea* tells the entrancing story of how one woman emerged from stagnation with the energy to persevere and the courage to re-create her life. This is a thoughtful, earthy recounting of an escape many women dream of—leaving familiar territory for a period of discovery and growth.

Joan Anderson and her husband married young, raised two sons, and lived in apparent harmony for over twenty years—he serving as the principal breadwinner, she fitting in writing projects and part-time careers around the major task of keeping the house and family running smoothly. Despite their happy appearance, however, Joan began to realize that she had unconsciously sacrificed important parts of herself in meeting the expectations placed on her as a traditional wife and mother. In an effort to break free of her unwanted roles, she decided to retreat to a family cottage for spiritual renewal. Out of that magical, difficult, transformational year came this book, a record of her experiences and a treasury of wisdom for readers.

Though Joan Anderson's year of self-discovery brought about extraordinary changes in her life, the steps that the author took to revitalize herself and rediscover her potential as an "unfinished woman" can help any woman release her own internal, untapped resources. Some readers may find themselves identifying with Joan when she realizes her long marriage just doesn't meet her emotional needs any longer, or share the familiar pang of self-doubt holding them back from full enjoyment of success.

Over the course of the year, Joan explores the seasons of Cape Cod while exploring her hidden self. Her adventures reveal the extraordinary resourcefulness and vitality of a seemingly ordinary woman. Although every woman must make her own journey toward self-discovery, *A Year by the Sea* offers a remarkable opportunity to find inspiration and wisdom in another's experience. One reader has compared this book to "an intimate conversation with a close friend." Some women have continued to explore Anderson's story through conversations with friends and groups of fellow readers. As you share the experience of reading this book with others, consider the following questions and exercises that address Anderson's inspiring story and how it can catalyze change in your own life.

QUESTIONS FOR DISCUSSION

1. At the beginning of the book, the author seems to leave her home, a familiar but outgrown place, without a great deal of anxiety about departing her old surroundings. By the end of *A Year by the Sea*, she has developed such a strong affinity for her cottage and small fishing town that she is unwilling to move anywhere else. How does the specific place where Anderson spends her year affect her outcome? In what ways would her discoveries have been different if she had spent the year in a city or other location?

2. The author has come to believe that all women should make it a priority to get away alone for two full days each year. Do you believe such a "sabbatical" would be helpful for every woman? How would you imagine spending two days alone, and what would you hope to take away from it?

3. In talking about the various forces shaping both her "old" and "new" lives, the author describes the restrictive expectations and requirements placed on her because of her gender and talks about limitations that women have faced in common. How have expectations on women, wives, and mothers changed since the Andersons' marriage began? Are women of all ages in the same peril of losing track of their innermost selves?

4. This book is subtitled *Thoughts of an Unfinished Woman*. In your own words, what does it mean to be an "unfinished woman"? Does the phrase have a positive or negative meaning for you? Do you fear the idea of being "finished,"

or does it seem like a welcome relief? Is being a fully realized person possible or even desirable?

5. Although she had made a living as a writer, the author chooses two jobs that require difficult manual labor over mental, creative tasks. Why do you believe she chose these two jobs? What do you think physical work can teach someone about herself?

6. The friendship with Joan Erikson was an important part of Anderson's year. Discuss the idea of a mentor, not only in a workplace but also in life.

7. Throughout the book, the author seeks spiritual refreshment and stillness beside the water and, at both the beginning and end of her year, she is moved by encounters with wild seals. What do you think the seals and water represent? Do they signal freedom from responsibility or joy, or something else?

8. How did you expect the Andersons' relationship to change as the story developed? Did you anticipate the way the book ended? How will the fruits of the author's year by the sea affect the relationship and, particularly, Joan's husband in the years to come?

9. Remember yourself at an earlier point in your life, and the dreams or expectations you held. Do your expectations from the past fit in with your present life? What small steps could you take to incorporate those dreams into your present life?

ABOUT THE AUTHOR

JOAN ANDERSON is a seasonal television and print journalist and author of several children's books, as well as of the critically acclaimed *Breaking the TV Habit*. She is a frequent speaker on women's issues and the role of the media in our lives. In an effort to share what she learned from her year by the sea, she has begun the popular "Weekend by the Sea" program, which is designed to help women reacquaint themselves with their feminine heritage, explore the bare essentials in simple living, and learn the act of being present.

OTHER READER'S COMPANIONS AVAILABLE

Alias Grace by Margaret Atwood

Art of the Personal Essay, The, edited by Phillip Lopate

Beach Music by Pat Conroy

Bodily Harm by Margaret Atwood

Bound Feet and Western Dress by Pang-Mei Natasha Chang

Cat's Eye by Margaret Atwood

Chitra Banerjee Divakaruni: About the Author and Her Works

Current Guide to Book Groups in the Workplace

Diary of a Young Girl: The Definitive Edition, The, by Anne Frank

Edible Woman, The, by Margaret Atwood

Everybody Was So Young by Amanda Vaill

Falling Leaves by Adeline Yen Mah

Hidden Writer, The, by Alexandra Johnson

Hope in the Unseen, A, by Ron Suskind

Ian McEwan: About the Author and His Works

In Defense of Elitism by William A. Henry III

J. California Cooper: About the Author and Her Works

Jane Hamilton (A Map of the World, The Book of Ruth)

Lady Oracle by Margaret Atwood

Language of Life, The, by Bill Moyers

Life Before Man by Margaret Atwood

Naguib Mafouz: About the Author and His Works

ORDERING INFORMATION

Reading group materials are available from Doubleday Broadway to support a vast array of interesting books. To obtain information on reading guides available from Doubleday Broadway, please call the Doubleday Broadway Marketing Hot Line at 1-800-605-3406, or visit us online at **www.randomhouse.com/resources**

All of our reading group companion guides are now available online at **www.randomhouse.com/resources/bookgroup** (subject to availability)

• • •

If you're interested in learning more about book groups—how to start one, how to join one, or what they're reading—find out all you need to know and more at our Book Group Corner on the Internet at
www.randomhouse.com/resources/bookgroup/

To contact Joan Anderson write to:

Box 1314
Harwich, Massachusetts 02645
email: joanleeand@webtv.net
Fax: 508 430-2820

Doubleday Broadway • 1540 Broadway • New York, New York 10036